ERMA BOMBECK

Writer and Humorist

Lynn Hutner Colwell

—Contemporary Women Series—

ENSLOW PUBLISHERS, INC.

Bloy St. and Ramsey Ave.	P.O. Box 38
Box 777	Aldershot
Hillside, N.J. 07205	Hants GU12 6BP
U.S.A.	U.K.

Library of Congress Cataloging-in-Publication Data

Colwell, Lynn Hutner.
   Erma Bombeck, writer and humorist / Lynn Hutner Colwell.
      p. cm. — (Contemporary women series)
   Includes bibliographical references (p.   ) and index.
   Summary: A biography of Erma Bombeck, tracing her life from her
early childhood in Dayton, Ohio, through her current life as one of
America's best-known humorists and columnists.
   ISBN 0-89490-384-5
   1. Bombeck, Erma—Biography—Juvenile literature. 2. Authors,
American—20th century—Biography—Juvenile literature.
3. Humorists, American—20th century—Biography—Juvenile
literature. [1. Bombeck, Erma. 2. Authors, American.
3. Humorists.] I. Title. II. Series.
PS3552.059Z63   1992
814'.54—dc20
[B]   91-40924
                                                          CIP
                                                           AC

Printed in the United States of America

10 9 8 7 6 5 4 3 2 1

Illustration Credits:
American Cancer Society, p. 98; Bowling Green State University Photo Services,
p. 10; Courtesy of Erma Bombeck, pp. 15, 17, 27, 37, 45, 65, 68, 69, 74, 101,
104; *Dayton Daily News*, pp. 24, 35, 40, 49, 50; Dept. of Archives and Special
Collections, Wright State University Library, pp. 14, 31; Jimmy Carter Library,
p. 71; Photo by Jim Marks, p. 83; Photo by Mike Goldman, p. 80; Universal
Press Syndicate, p. 6.

Cover Illustration: Tom Arma/Outline Press

Contents

Acknowledgements

Writing a biography is not a one-person job. I am most grateful to Gladys Justin Carr and Aaron Priest for their insights; to Dawn Dewey of Wright State University; to Michael Passo, director of the Dayton Newspapers, Inc., Reference Library, and the many other people who so diligently searched for pictures to complement the story; to Tracy Devine for her persistence; to Norma Born for help with the details; and, of course, to Erma Bombeck for sharing family photos, memories, and a great ham sandwich.

Lynn Hutner Colwell

Erma Bombeck

Introduction

Four writers turn out 99 percent of the written humor that's gobbled up along with toast and coffee in most American homes each morning. They are the people who "write funny"—humorists who spin yarns for newspapers across the country. It may be coincidence that all four boast last names beginning with the letter "B"—Art Buchwald, Russell Baker, Dave Barry, and Erma Bombeck—but it wasn't coincidence that turned a shy Ohio teenager into one of America's funniest and best-loved writers.

Erma Bombeck, like millions of other writers, has talent. She's creative, intuitive, and she'll even admit to being lucky. But most of all, she loves to write. Erma loves to write the way youngsters love their puppies, the way teenagers love their cars, the way parents love their kids. And because she loves it so much, work that others might find tedious or boring keeps her springing from her bed each morning, fingers itching to attack the typewriter.

She seems, to an outsider's view, extraordinarily self-disciplined. For twenty-five years she's produced enough humor to fill three newspaper columns a week—over 3,200 columns total. In a quarter of a century, she's missed only one deadline. When she's not writing columns, Erma's producing books. As quickly as the publisher can turn them out, they top the bestseller lists. They've been translated into more than a dozen languages, and every one of her humor books has sold at least 500,000 copies in hardcover. No other nonfiction writer comes close to matching her consistent popular success.

Besides penning best-sellers, Erma has lectured, written a television series, and scripted eleven years' worth of appearances on *Good Morning America*. She's raised three children as well as hundreds of thousands of dollars for charity.

For years, until she wore herself out, she worked seven days a week. Even now, she takes only four weeks off from column writing each year. The rest of the time she's glued to her desk from early morning until late afternoon, agonizing over words and punctuation, endlessly fine-tuning the combinations that will make people laugh.

Erma Bombeck's road to fame and fortune was paved with plain old-fashioned hard work. She's worked despite illness that hospitalized her and kids who held her hostage to carpools.

There were never any shortcuts.

Erma's family had little money while she was growing up. When her father died, Erma was nine and her mother went to work full-time. There's a saying that humor arises from suffering, that people who have endured traumatic or painful years as children turn that inside out and become the comedians of the world. Erma disagrees. Although others might call her deprived, she remembers a happy, fun-filled, adventurous childhood peppered with ups and downs. She never understood how poor and unfortunate she was.

As a youngster, Erma devoured books the way other children gobble up candy. She was so quiet that when she became famous, some of her childhood classmates had a hard time remembering her face. Although she had friends, she never quite felt a part of the crowd. Losing her father set her apart, but even before that, she observed life as much as she lived it. The lifelong habit of watching people and absorbing their personal qualities and behaviors invigorates her writing and makes readers exclaim, "She's writing about me!"

Some people claim that Erma's fans are limited to a small, avid group of women readers. Nothing could be farther from the truth. Although Erma has championed the cause of stay-at-home women, even the feminist and syndicated columnist Ellen Goodman admits to needing a periodic dose of Erma's wit. "No matter how much I've changed, my toilet's still going to leak," Goodman explains. Men and young people crowd her infrequent lectures. Cary Grant, a world-famous actor, was an admirer. Shirley Temple Black, probably the most beloved child movie star of all time and later ambassador to Ghana, once proclaimed that the people she most admired were First Lady Eleanor Roosevelt and Erma Bombeck.

People appreciate Bombeckian humor because it is based on the natural inclination to laugh at circumstances beyond their control. Erma's wit offers insights into our evolving culture. Her satire combines keen observations about life's absurdities with a skillful use of language. And just as her three children have matured, so has her writing. Early on, she depended on one-liners to hook and reel in her audience. She feared people wouldn't accept her more reflective thoughts. It took a long time for her confidence to build, to reach the point where she could balance the dark and light sides of life. Today, her words inevitably touch the funny bone—and the heart.

It's important to Erma that people understand she is an ordinary person. She never claimed to be the most brilliant woman who ever lived. Just the opposite. In interviews and casual conversation, she tends to put herself down. But it's not inborn talent we see reflected in her words. It's the motivated, self-disciplined workaholic who won't quit for the day until the perfect phrase springs from the page.

Erma took a natural inclination and turned it into a passion that continues to intrigue her into her sixth decade of life.

Erma's work has not gone unrewarded. In addition to making a good living from her words, she has received more than a dozen honorary degrees from colleges and universities across the country. She's inspired thousands of young people at graduations by stressing the principles that underlie her life: respect for others, high expectations, and, naturally, a sense of humor.

And Erma Bombeck's success has never gone to her head. Looking at her today, it's easy to picture the unsophisticated teenager she was, decked out in bobby socks and plaid skirt, with a barrette in her hair. She's famous, but she's as down-to-earth as your mother. When the paperback rights to one of her early books

Bowling Green State University honored Erma in 1978 with a Doctor of Humane Letters degree.

sold for $1 million, she celebrated like any unspoiled housewife would have. She didn't do the laundry for three days.

Erma lives in a house that clings to the side of a mountain in Paradise Valley, Arizona. It has a pool and a tennis court, but it's not the neighborhood showplace. Inside, it's homey. A bunch of chatty birds occupy a chandelier turned cage in a corner of the dining room. Knickknacks crowd the shelves. It's the kind of house where you feel at home as soon as you walk in.

Erma is like that herself. She dislikes being a celebrity. She'd rather just be Erma, joking with her kids, whipping up a casserole for a few friends, or lobbing tennis balls over the net at her lifelong companion, husband Bill.

But because she's famous, Erma believes people expect a lot from her. Take her size. She's five feet two inches tall. But whenever she greets someone new, she senses disillusionment. "They expect me to be taller," she says seriously. You can tell she's sorry to disappoint them.

Insecurity has been a part of Erma's makeup as long as she can remember. She admires well-known people who walk in and light up a room, who remember to remove the pacifiers from their purses before their kids graduate from college, and who never greet dignitaries with runs in their stockings.

New acquaintances, Erma believes, expect her to "act" funny. "She thinks she's hysterical. Big deal. I could have said that," she imagines people muttering to themselves.

And maybe they could, but no one consistently tickles our funnybones like Erma Bombeck.

Leaky toilets, leaky toddlers, newly licensed teenagers, giving birth, getting even, slow husbands, slower cars, hair, teeth, fingers and toes, too fat, too thin, too anything at all, new-fangled gadgets or old-fashioned love. Whatever the situation, Erma Bombeck steers her readers through the difficult waters of life with nothing more substantial than laughter. But then, what else do we need?

Many well-known people, once they have more money than they need and more fame than they can handle, quietly slip from sight. They give up whatever brought them the astonishing income and the recognition and live out their days surrounded by memories. People often ask Erma, "You're so successful. Why continue the grind? Why not quit and take it easy?"

Partly it's because writing to Erma has become as natural and as necessary as breathing. The other part? Magic. The magic of words that can bring people to tears, stir laughter, awaken the deep, secret feelings we're too shy to share. Erma gets a kick from knowing her words affect people, give them a lift, and sometimes make them think.

She doesn't want to give that up.

And as long as she's around anyway, bewildered by the oddities of modern life, Erma can't see staying silent. After all, who else would point out that Miss America never sweats or that you will never own a car that outlasts the payments, or admit that housework, if you do it right, will kill you?

Who else but Erma Bombeck?

1

Early Childhood

Erma Bombeck was born to make people laugh. But the circumstances she was born into were not very funny. Her mother, also named Erma, had grown up in an orphanage, attended school only through the fourth grade, and, at the age of fourteen, married Cassius Edwin Fiste, who was seventeen years her senior. Erma Louise Fiste was born on February 21, 1927—when her own mother was just sixteen years old.

With her parents and half-sister Thelma, Erma lived on Hedges Street in a Dayton, Ohio, neighborhood filled with hardworking, lower middle class families. Her dad, a crane operator for the city of Dayton, couldn't offer the family many extras, but Erma never remembers feeling poor. There was always food on the table, serviceable clothing, and enough money squeezed out each month to pay for tap dancing lessons.

Erma's mother, like millions of other American moms of the time, dreamed that the girls would one day be as famous as Shirley Temple. Shirley, the singing, dancing child movie star who made her film debut at the age of three, tapped her way through the thirties starring in a string of musical hits. Erma and Shirley were almost the same age. But while Shirley's dimpled smile reflected her sunny, outgoing nature, Erma admits that she was painfully shy. Shyness, however, was not a problem in her mother's eyes. Mrs. Fiste believed this small character flaw would be overcome once Erma learned to dance.

She started tap lessons at the age of five. Erma claims she wasn't very good, but she soon landed a spot in the *Kiddie Review*, a local radio show. Strange as it sounds, in those days tap dancers displayed their talents on local radio shows. Although only the studio audience could see them, the girls were made up, costumed, and performed as though a million people were poised to applaud. Erma stayed on the program for eight years.

Even when they weren't dancing, Erma and Thelma were a

Erma's hometown of Dayton, Ohio in 1929.

By age nine, Erma was a tap dancing pro.

team. Erma idolized her sister, who was seven years older. On weekends when Thelma visited her natural mother, Erma would sit, chin in hands, on the front steps of the house for hours, peering up and down the street, eagerly awaiting her big sister's return.

The two girls liked to gang up on their parents. They enjoyed jokes and silly stunts. If their mother put the bed on one side of the room, they would get up in the middle of the night and move it to the other. They giggled at the confusion on their mother's face when she woke them in the morning, and each vigorously denied having anything to do with the mysterious redecoration. Despite the difference in their ages, the girls stood up for each other. Erma could talk to Thelma about anything. She could also talk her into anything. Erma often avoided doing the dishes by convincing Thelma to take on the dreaded chore. For nine years, the stepsisters shared their lives and forged a strong bond between them, one that was to shatter with the sudden death of their father, Cassius Fiste.

At the age of five, Erma ached to attend school. With Thelma away all day, Erma was bored. Although children generally did not begin first grade until they were six, Erma's eagerness along with her mother's certainty that she was ready, convinced the principal to admit her.

She couldn't yet read, but Erma had already fallen in love with books. She raced around the house, collecting all the volumes she could find and toted them off to school.

There was nothing unusual about Erma's family in those days. Her dad left early and returned home, during the winter, when the sky had already started to darken. He would tell Erma to get her bicycle off the sidewalk before someone fell over it. She always forgot. Her mother cleaned the house, cooked the meals, and saw to it that the girls left home neatly dressed in the morning. It was all very ordinary, very normal until the day when Erma was nine and her father collapsed and died of a stroke.

Until then, Erma had really never thought much about her

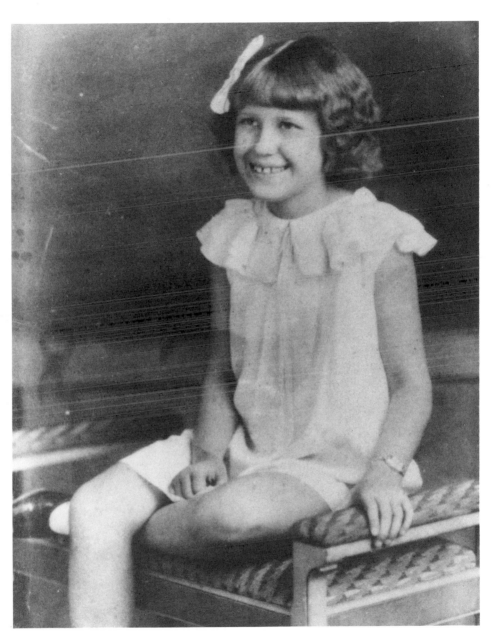

Erma as a child, her shyness hidden behind a smile.

father. She had taken him for granted. He was like a shadow, wandering about on the edges of her life. She thought him brave because he was the only one in the family who wasn't afraid to go into the basement by himself, and she loved him dearly, without understanding how or why.

People swarmed through the house and patted Erma on the head as if she had done something special. She'd never had so much attention before from other people. She liked it. She did feel sad, but mostly she felt a longing to know what would happen next. How would all this affect her?

She quickly found out when she went back to school a few days later. Something had changed. Her schoolmates treated her differently. Most of them had never been to a funeral. Certainly, they had not lost a father. She sensed a wary respect, but a pulling away too. It was as if she had recently recovered from a nameless disease that the other children feared they might catch.

Not too long after her father died, men came and removed all the furniture from the house, even Erma's bed and dresser. The furnishings hadn't been fully paid for, and the company took them back. Still Erma didn't worry. She would be moving to a new neighborhood to live in her grandparents' home, and she was looking forward to it.

And when, one day, Thelma packed her cardboard suitcase and headed for the streetcar, Erma hardly said good-bye. Consumed with excitement about her own future, Erma had no idea that she would not see her beloved sister again for eight years.

Erma and her mother left the residential area in which they had lived and moved to a more commercial part of the city. Dayton's hundreds of industries had attracted immigrants from many foreign countries. In the thirties, the population boasted sizable representations of Hungarians, Rumanians, Poles, Lithuanians, Dutch, Greeks, Italians, Turks, Croatians, Bulgarians, Russians, and Serbs. Erma's grandmother's house sat in the middle of a multiethnic neighborhood. She lived near a synagogue, a Catholic church, and Protestant churches among a lively mix of Italians, Irish, and Jews. A revival tent swayed on one corner, a bar stood on another. A theater and a candy store lay just beyond the doorstep.

Erma's best friend lived over a funeral parlor, and for entertainment the girls attended the synagogue on Saturday and the Catholic church on Sunday. It didn't matter that they were Protestants. They rejoiced in the music and the ceaseless chatter of languages they couldn't understand.

The home of Erma's grandparents boasted almost as odd a cast of characters as the neighborhood. The grandparents had two unmarried children, a son who played pool all day and was out all night, and Aunt Martha who cleaned houses for a living. Another daughter, Aunt Louise, her husband, and two children moved in, bringing the total to ten relatives spreading through the house.

Erma and her mother shared the front bedroom for two years. With Thelma gone, the two Ermas united against the world. Because her mother was so young, they related well and enjoyed each other's company. Erma never felt misplaced in the midst of her rather bizarre surroundings, but when her mother went to work, Erma missed her a lot.

The young, widowed Mrs. Fiste found her first job at the Leland Electric Factory. Later she worked at a General Motors plant, where she inserted the rubber strips around car doors.

The only child in her class whose mother worked outside the home, Erma didn't tell anyone but her best friend, who got mad at her and spread it around the school.

When her mother left for work each morning, Erma felt deserted. The ten-year-old no longer rested comfortably in the center of her mother's world, and she missed the attention. But her feelings didn't stop her from enjoying school. She was an eager student and, at least until difficulties surfaced in college, an excellent one. She delighted in books from an early age. Reading opened up life to her

19

and helped her cope with the world of adults in which she found herself. With her mother working, she spent a lot of time alone. She learned to live with herself. Television didn't exist. When the school day ended, she would rush home, grab a book, and scramble to her special spot under the eves where it was cool. She would read out loud taking all the parts as though she were in a play. At Christmas, while her friends begged for dolls and bikes, she pleaded for books. Stories about foreign correspondents fired her imagination. While Erma claims she was never an unhappy child, reading provided an escape to a world she certainly found more exciting if not more pleasant.

Once Erma fell in love with stories and words, she quickly realized that a very different life existed beyond Bainbridge Street. She understood that she would never fulfill her mother's dream. She didn't want to be a tap dancer. She wanted to make up stories and write for the school newspaper. English became the only subject she cared about. Every other period in the school day became just another hour to get through. She longed to travel and experience life beyond Dayton. And even at the age of ten, she wanted to write about it.

2

Growing Up

When Erma was eleven, her mother married Albert (Tom) Harris. "If you think you're going to take my father's place, you're crazy," Erma thundered at her new stepfather. Even though her hardworking mother was just twenty-seven and deserved a better life, Erma could only see her own place being lost to this stranger. She felt jealous and sorry for herself. For a while, she would talk to Tom only through her mother. He thought the child needed discipline, and he dished it out. Erma responded with the standard stepchild's retort, "You can't tell me what to do. You're not my real father!"

Tom made an effort to understand his new stepdaughter, but she didn't make it easy. He had entered into a first marriage with an older woman (he was three years younger than Erma's mother) and took on fathering not an infant, but a stubborn preteen. The fact that Erma strongly resembled her father probably didn't help.

But eventually, Erma realized that both she and Tom loved her mother. They settled into a fragile, uneasy peace. Polite but distant, Erma held no deep feelings toward Tom until years later, after her own children had been born. Then suddenly, she began to understand what Tom did, he had to do—that he had done it out of love.

The new family moved into their own home on Oak Street. Situated in the same kind of neighborhood they had left, the house was unremarkable except for one feature. It was the only house within the Dayton city limits featuring a toilet perched on the porch. The toilet occupied a tiny enclosed room, but it might as well have stood under a billboard with an arrow pointing straight down. Everybody in the neighborhood knew Erma's house.

At school, Erma played the bookworm. Class clown? Definitely not. But if anyone had cared to search beneath the surface, they would have discovered a child fascinated by humor. Erma practically inhaled the works of popular humorists including Robert Benchley, James Thurber, and H. Allen Smith. So it's not surprising that when given the opportunity to write for the school newspaper, she produced a humor column. The staff of Emerson Junior High allowed the newspaper, *The Owl,* to carry Erma's work even though it was biting and sometimes even cruel. Perhaps someone spotted her talent, but more likely they burst out laughing at her descriptions of inedible lunches, arrogant teachers, and trouble-making students. With those first columns, Erma discovered the power of words. Some teachers took her columns so seriously that she was threatened with expulsion, but others accepted the needling and even praised her. Praise from teachers and students fueled her desire to poke fun at the world. The columns she writes today are more mature, deeper, better written, but they trace their roots to the eighth grade at Emerson Junior High.

When she moved on to Patterson Vocational High School, Erma crammed school, social, and academic news into her own column. It was basically serious stuff, but she always managed to fit in at least one amusing tidbit like this: "In sociology class, it is discovered that there is no teacher worse than your fellow students. The sisters [teaching nuns] have given over the class to the students . . .

Results: If you have a blank look on your face, you're a dead ringer to be called upon."

Patterson Vocational High School operated on a unique system. Students alternated two weeks attending school with two weeks working in a real-life setting. Classes ran from 8:00 A.M. until 4:00 P.M. with two weeks off in the summer. The system suited Erma perfectly. Not only did she land her first newspaper job as a high school sophomore, but she learned to type well and take shorthand, skills she would use throughout her life.

Most of Erma's teachers thought of her as quiet and conscientious. She made no waves, no mistakes, never called attention to herself. Hiding behind her pen, Erma wrote school plays but never appeared in them.

But journalism class was different. Erma was named features editor on the school paper and wrote her own bylined column. She felt comfortable with teacher Jim Harris. As a result, the hidden Erma emerged—an outgoing teenager with an engaging sense of humor. Years later, when Erma became a "public" figure, this was the side she showed the world because this is what the world demanded. Few people realized that Erma still considers the shy, insecure side to be the more genuine part of her character. But throughout her life, Erma has made insecurity work for her. Early on, she recognized her shortcomings. She wasn't the smartest, the thinnest, or the richest. She worried a lot. And most of the time she felt terribly inadequate. But instead of crying over what she was missing, Erma accepted her weaknesses and built on her strengths.

One day when she was fifteen, she walked into the office of the managing editor of the *Dayton Journal-Herald,* the city's daily newspaper and said, "I want to work for your paper." The editor explained that only a full-time position was available.

"That's O.K. I can work two weeks and get you another girl to work the two weeks I'm in school. While she's in school, I'll work.

That's how our school operates. It'll be just like having a full-time person," Erma ended triumphantly. She was hired.

If high school was fun for Erma, the newspaper was heaven. In those days no unions limited which employees could perform what tasks for how many hours a day. Erma did mostly whatever no one else wanted to do or had time to. She mixed paste, sorted mail, cleaned anything that needed it, jogged six blocks to pick up the foreign editions just in from exotic locales like Paris and Chicago, and delivered them to the editorial writers. She ran errands, scribbled phone messages, even took the editor's suits to the cleaners. And she loved it all. She thrived on the bustle, the noise, the excitement that vibrated right down to her bones. A newspaper is a

Seventeen-year-old Erma and the staff of the *Dayton Journal-Herald.*

living, breathing thing. It's a place where something is always happening. Erma felt as though she had a seat on the fifty-yard line. She thought she worked in the most exciting building in the world and that writing for a newspaper must be the best job anyone could ever have.

She proudly wore the title "copygirl," but Erma wrote for the newspaper only once during high school. In a humorous twist of fate (although her mother didn't share Erma's amusement), Shirley Temple came to Dayton for the premiere of her latest movie, *Since You Went Away*. Erma interviewed her as one sixteen-year-old to another, and the story was published on the feature page. Erma received the newspaper staff award for feature of the week—$10 and a spot on the bulletin board. That day, she assured herself, marked the beginning of a great career.

The dating game was shy one player in Erma Fiste. During her high school years, she felt so insecure that she could hardly imagine dating. She considered herself terribly plain and unattractive. When she was around boys, she overcame her shyness by tossing off sharp-witted remarks and put-downs. She thought that if she could ever find a guy who could put up with her outspoken humor, there might be some hope. But Erma entertained no thoughts of settling in with some sweet-faced, wishy-washy boy anyway. She was intent on being herself, on calling the shots and being in control. The seeds of feminism were born then in a young girl who refused to be placed in a neat little mold. Erma didn't want to play the game. She shunned flirting and avoided girls who allowed guys to win. None of it seemed right to her. She felt strongly that women were as intelligent as men but that social circumstances held them back. She resented the idea that society considered men to be superior to women in every way—physically, mentally, and emotionally.

There was one boy, though. He worked for the morning paper, the *Dayton Journal*. When copygirl met copyboy, sparks flew, at least for Erma. Bill Bombeck attended the Catholic high school, and he played the field—when he wasn't going steady with one of a half-dozen girls. Erma thought he was gorgeous. She didn't care if he couldn't put two words together and come up with a sentence. She eyed him for two or three years before they got together. Then, after only a couple of dates, he left for the Army and Korea.

As her senior year approached, Erma began thinking about her future. She desperately wanted to go to college, but her after-school job at a dress shop would barely cover the application, much less finance tuition. Besides, her parents were opposed to the idea. In lower middle class families, education was considered a luxury, college a place where wealthy girls hunted husbands. Erma was expected to finish eighth grade, then get a job. Just about everyone else in her family had done that. Unmarried young people lived at home, paid for room and board, and helped out financially to the tune of a good part of their salaries. After junior high came payback time. Erma's parents felt they had been more than generous in allowing her to attend high school.

But Erma knew she wouldn't be ready to pay back for quite a while. She wanted more out of life than a salesgirl's salary and a high school education. While her parents' opposition presented problems, lack of money appeared to be the biggest obstacle blocking Erma's dream. She wasn't about to let that stop her.

Graduating from high school in 1944 and determined to build a college fund, Erma assumed two full-time jobs. After three years as a copygirl, the *Dayton Journal-Herald* hired her as a full-time writer. The job relieved her of the menial labor she had been performing, but there was little opportunity to win a Pulitzer Prize for journalism. She spent most of the stint writing obituaries. Toward the end of the year, she was promoted to radio scheduling. And while it may not have been the most stimulating work, Erma could hardly wait to get out of bed in the morning and dash to the paper. It felt good to be a part of something so vital. The longer

Erma as she looked upon graduation from high school.

Erma worked at the newspaper, the more she understood the importance of every job. From managing editor to obituary writer to the kids who delivered the paper—still smelling of ink—to hundreds of front porches every day, each helped bring the news to life. Erma felt proud of the role she played.

At night, she edited proofs of airplane manuals at Wright-Patterson Air Force Base. The *Dayton Journal-Herald* paid $20 a week and the evening job quite a bit more. Erma gave her parents $5 a week to cover room and board and saved the rest. After a year of working night and day, her savings account held enough to launch her college career. Although she could have stayed in Dayton, she chose instead to begin experiencing life on her own at Ohio University in Athens, 137 miles from home.

After working four years at the *Dayton Journal-Herald,* Erma had become a favorite. Everyone knew and admired her for working so hard to improve herself. People were anxious to help her fulfill her dream, not only to go to college, but also to enjoy the experience as any young person should. When Erma was ready to leave for school, many who had grown to love her like a sister or daughter came forward with contributions to show their support. One gave Erma her old portable typewriter. Others offered clothes and luggage. They took up a collection so she could come home at Christmas. The women on the staff donated enough money so that she could attend sorority rush parties. Even though they knew she couldn't afford to join, they didn't want her deprived of the fun.

Although Erma had more real-world working experience than most people her age, the first semester of college proved a disaster. Maybe it was just a matter of being away from home for the first time. There was so much to absorb. It occurred to her from time to time that she just wasn't smart enough. She couldn't seem to figure out what the professors wanted her to do. In high school, her writing had been praised. She had been told she could write, yet she barely passed first semester freshman composition at the university. She argued with her professor about what constituted good literature and pulled a "C" in his course. Hoping to work for the school newspaper, which enjoyed an excellent reputation, she submitted several articles that were all rejected. She had worked with a newspaper for four years, but her writing wasn't good enough to land her a staff job on a college paper.

Hurt and confused, Erma visited an academic counselor. "What is it that you'd like to do with your life?" he asked. Erma replied that she wanted to be a writer. Surveying her first semester grades, he said firmly, "Don't." Erma was stunned.

Although she had always suffered from feelings of inadequacy, she had never before questioned her ability to overcome them. Now wounded and discouraged, Erma wondered where she was heading. She had fought her parents for the right to an education. Besides going to school, she worked to support herself. She had secured a good job with three doctors in the science department. She hadn't asked anyone for help. People at the newspaper believed in her, supported her. Had she come this far only to fail at the one thing she had ever wanted?

And she wondered, "If I can't write, what am I going to do with my life?"

Her parents, she knew, wanted her to quit. She desperately needed to prove to them that they were wrong, that she could earn a living writing. Her mother's hopes for Erma had been dashed when, after graduating from high school, she never picked up her tap shoes again. Erma's mother thought writing was boring. Where was the glamour? She wanted to see her daughter's face gracing the covers of movie magazines. Bylines rarely generated interest, much less fame. She didn't change her mind until the night, twenty years later, when Erma appeared on the *Tonight Show*.

Erma was depressed by her initiation into college life and by her money situation. When her mother asked her to come home, Erma packed her things, gave up her job, and returned to Dayton.

She felt defeated. For the first time in her life, her naturally sunny nature took a vacation. For most students, college marks the best years of their lives. For Erma, it meant little but struggle.

Living at home meant dealing with the typical mother-daughter struggles that mark many similar relationships. While Erma and her mother were close, they could not have been more different. Coming at every situation from opposite angles, they disagreed on almost every subject. Their lives became a tug-of-war. At a time when Erma craved support, she also needed independence. How could she help pushing her mother away? She felt like a rebel, but worse, with nothing but negative input from everyone around her, she feared she might end up a failure. Maybe after all, they would turn out to be right.

Fueled by an intense desire to prove herself, Erma enrolled at the University of Dayton, a private, medium-sized four-year Catholic college. She continued to struggle financially, but found a writing outlet when she tackled a job with Rike's department store, where she joked about clearance sales, the lunch menu, and even shoplifting in their employee newsletter.

During her sophomore year at Dayton, Erma finally found someone who believed in her talent and restored some of her shattered self-confidence. Brother Tom Price had read some articles she had produced for the school newspaper and asked her to write for the university's magazine, *The Exponent.* At night, when she returned from work, she'd sit at the typewriter and crank out the copy. Psychology and philosophy courses expanded her understanding of the people she observed and gave her writing more depth and sensitivity.

One day, after reading one of her articles, Tom Price turned to Erma and said the three words that would sustain her for the rest of her career. "You can write," he said, "you can write."

By pinching every penny, Erma scraped by until the last semester of her senior year. Then the money ran out. She didn't have the $144 tuition. She asked the registrar if she could monitor classes and pay the tuition later. He said no. After four and a half years of college combined with working to support herself, she was exhausted. Working her way through school meant Erma had missed out on the social and extracurricular activities that help young people grow and mature in positive ways. She felt tired. The diploma didn't mean that much to her anymore. She decided to quit.

Occasionally while she was in college, her mother had given Erma small amounts of money. She was more understanding than Erma cared to admit. So Erma was shocked when she shared her

Rike's department store in Dayton, where Erma worked to earn money for college.

decision with her mother. "You've come this far," her mother said. "You might as well finish." And she loaned Erma the money.

Erma took the loan, but felt angry. She hadn't enjoyed college the way she thought she deserved to, and she blamed a lot of her unhappiness on her parents. Blinded by her own feelings, she ignored her mother's good intentions. Besides, she deeply resented needing help after coming so far on her own. When Erma received her diploma, she dropped it in her mother's lap and snapped, "You wanted it. Now you've got it." To this day, she regrets those words.

3

A Typical Fifties Housewife

More educated now than any previous member of her family had ever been, Erma willingly abandoned academic life and dove back into the newspaper business. The *Dayton Journal-Herald* welcomed her home. She was assigned to the women's section.

In those days, it was assumed women lacked curiosity about the national debt, politics, or anything international unless it was a recipe. Their interests supposedly lay within easy reach of their apron strings—children, gardening, cooking, and etiquette. Many female reporters, destined to spend years turning out "fluff," longed to move to the city side of newspapers, where reporters dealt with important issues of the day. Women's departments were a bit of a joke, and no one was more aware of it than the women themselves. While there were a few women on the city side, for the most part, female reporters' stories rarely made the front page. If they wanted to try something creative or different, they were told there was no time or no space. They battled to squeeze new angles from photographers who were quite happy to line up four apron-clad women and snap a photo as they stared at a light bulb.

The unfair treatment frustrated Erma, but she rarely complained.

If she did, it was to another woman, certainly not to anyone in power. Besides, the smell of the newsroom, the clatter of the wires, and the shirt-sleeved reporters chomping unlit cigars and typing their stories like frantic squirrels fighting a winter deadline made her feel alive. This was what she had craved for so long. It was as if she had never been gone. She hoped some day to be promoted to the city side, but there was no rush. If she gave her best to every assignment, no matter how dull or silly she found the subject, she assumed that eventually she'd earn a move across the hall.

Erma wrote mostly on assignment. The editor would ask her to grab the story on this week's meeting of the garden club or chat with the oldest living woman in Dayton. But she was encouraged to pitch her own ideas too. She remembers stopping in the doorway of John Moore's office. Moore was the managing editor for whom she'd worked when she was in high school. He motioned for her to enter and take a seat. Erma sat. Moore's foot, propped on his desk as he casually polished his shoe, blocked her view. After a minute of silence, Erma stood up and said, "I'm not going to pitch an idea with your feet in my face." Her bold stance may have surprised Moore, but it proved that Erma possessed enough self-confidence to risk angering her boss.

While her work turned out to have some negatives, her love life had taken a decided turn for the better. After Bill Bombeck, whom Erma had met at the newspaper, left for Korea during the final stages of World War II, the two corresponded. Erma's letters impressed Bill. When he returned to Dayton, they began dating seriously.

Bill spent Christmas Eve 1948 at Erma's home. They had grown so close that Erma was half expecting a marriage proposal. But as the evening wore on and Bill seemed as relaxed as usual, Erma assumed she had been wrong. Around midnight, Bill casually lit up a cigar. Erma grumbled and tried to wave the smoke away. Then she caught sight of something. Her engagement ring hung from the

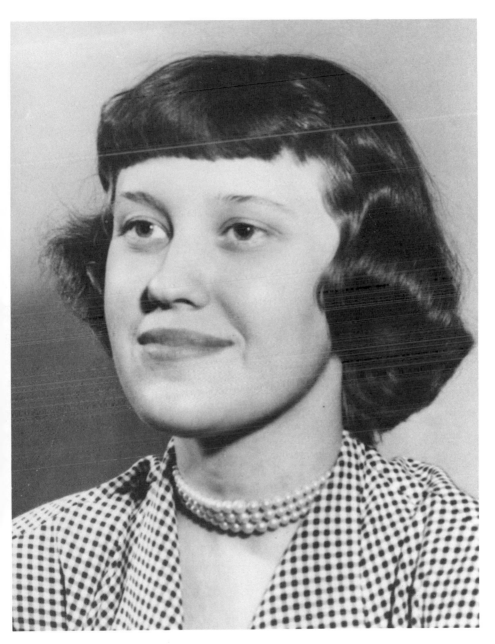

Twenty-three-year-old Erma, a journalist at last.

end of the cigar—a comically romantic touch that endeared Bill to Erma forever. In Bill, Erma found a soul mate with a sense of humor as sharp as her own; a man who could see through her sarcasm and retorts to a shy, sensitive woman who needed the love he offered. Today Erma and Bill wear matching gold cigar-band rings just in case either should ever forget their romantic beginnings.

Prior to their wedding, Erma converted from the United Brethren Church to Roman Catholicism. It was an independent act, but not a defiant one. The rituals of the Catholic Church moved her. She wanted to be part of a religion rich in culture and history.

The Bombecks, both age twenty-two, were married at the Church of the Resurrection on an overcast morning in August. Erma had never felt as beautiful as she did at her wedding. She wore an elegant organza gown, a bargain she could never have afforded without the generosity of the buyer from Rike's department store who offered the dress at a large discount. It wasn't her size, but the store seamstress, a romantic woman who had known Erma and wanted to make her special day perfect, altered the dress for free.

One hundred and fifty people—mostly Erma's relatives—attended the wedding, which was uneventful except for a bridesmaid who fell into a dead faint halfway through the Mass. She hadn't eaten that morning and had no idea the service would last so long. The newlyweds borrowed a car from Bill's sister and drove to Sunny Lake Ranch in Michigan for a brief honeymoon.

They had rented an apartment on Holly Avenue, and when they returned, Bill plunged into his last year at the University of Dayton while Erma continued at the paper. She took her work seriously, but wasn't beyond playing a practical joke now and then. Editor Marj Heyduck was a joy to work for. But Marj was out of the office a lot. Being a columnist, she didn't stick to regular hours. She'd take off early and come in late. "Where's Marj?" got to be a running joke around the *Dayton Journal-Herald* office.

One day as a joke, Erma wrote Marj's obituary. It must have

On her wedding day, Erma looked and felt like a beautiful bride.

sounded real enough because someone picked it up, put it in the basket, sent it down the chute, and set it in type. The obit ran in the first edition. Marj thought it was hysterical. Erma almost lost her job.

Erma returned to writing humor in 1952. At first her columns, which ran under the title "Operation Dustrag," offered household hints and new product evaluations. Then newlywed Erma discovered housework. Household absurdities quickly found their way into the column.

The newspapers' editors viewed her work skeptically. Newspapers were supposed to offer news. A humor column? No one was certain that purposefully amusing writing belonged in the paper. Besides, in those days, no one attacked homemaking—in the newspaper or anywhere else. Running a home was considered an art. When your laundry was whiter than your neighbor's, you felt superior for a week. Preparing just-baked cookies and a glass of milk for the children when they returned from school and scrubbing the corners of the kitchen floor with a toothbrush were considered necessary to domestic survival. A clean home and cleaner children gave a woman status. No one had ever questioned the necessity of such work before. No one had taken an irreverent look at the homefront before Erma Bombeck.

At the same time, World War II had created a profound change for American women. With their men at war, millions of women flooded the workplace—75 percent of them were married and one-third had children under the age of fourteen. At the war's end, most returned to the nest but were left with lingering doubts. They had enjoyed dressing up each day and having somewhere to go, liked getting a paycheck. They began to question whether they had been born to spend their lives cutting meat into small pieces and ironing shoelaces. They had sipped freedom, and they liked the taste.

Erma's first columns struck a nerve with these women. The

newspaper editors had anticipated receiving complaints. Positive comments outnumbered the negative, but the people at the top still felt uneasy. The time for publicly spoofing domestic life had not yet arrived.

And while Erma joked about family life and the terrors kids inflict on the home scene, she desperately wanted a child of her own. She had no idea at the time that the scenes of domestic chaos she described in those early columns would one day bring her the fame and fortune her mother had envisioned as she hauled Erma to tap dancing lessons in her childhood. By the age of twenty-five, Erma had worked nearly half her life. She was tired of the routine and longed for the domestic scenes she had already begun to satirize.

Bill had taken a job as a science teacher at Centerville High School. They bought their first car, a 1938 Plymouth, for $150 and a piece of land in a nice neighborhood on the edge of town where they built a tiny house, all they could afford at the time. Unfortunately, neighbors petitioned the city to get rid of the house because "it didn't suit the character of the area," meaning it wasn't as large as others in the community. Since the home met area restrictions, it stayed. But the experience erased some of the excitement Bill and Erma felt at owning their first home.

For two years, the young couple tried to have a baby. Their doctor confirmed that chances of Erma's conceiving were small, and they decided to adopt. After filling out boxes full of forms and meeting with social workers whose job it was to insure that they would provide a stable, loving home for a child, they waited. Finally, Erma received a call from a Catholic Services social worker. She was about to become a mother. The call signaled a temporary end to a vital part of Erma's life. With no hesitation, she traded the familiar scent of newsprint for the sweet perfume of a newborn baby girl.

Erma lived up to a pact she had made with God. "Give me

Erma about a year before she left the *Dayton Journal-Herald* to become a full-time mother.

children, and I'll stay home and take care of them," she had silently promised. When Betsy came into her life, she said goodbye to her career and the people she had grown up with at the newspaper without the slightest doubt that she was doing the right thing. Erma plunged into motherhood with the same enthusiasm she had brought to writing. She loved being a mother—even though she often felt inadequate and uncertain.

Erma became a mother and a housewife at a time when firm social standards defined both. While a mother might work outside of the house, her activity was considered "unimportant." Most married women who worked did so out of necessity. It was a substantial point of pride for middle class men to support their families without their wives having to resort to working out the home.

The ideal mother of the fifties directed, supervised, and nurtured her children. Their needs came first, hers last—if at all. Women were constantly reminded that child raising was the most important activity they could perform. By carrying out all the tasks of child care and household upkeep, women were supposed to feel completely fulfilled.

Some did. But many others felt shock and guilt when they discovered that caring for children and housework weren't enough. They adored their children and enjoyed many of the activities associated with raising them, yet they often felt empty and depressed. Isolated from other adults, they worked at repetitive tasks for which there was little reward and less recognition. Society publicly applauded motherhood and housewifely duties on one hand and invested it with no real value on the other.

No one assumed that "anyone" could be a doctor. But "anyone" could be a housewife and mother. People who earned the most respect in society generally earned the most money. Housewives earned nothing. The world's best casserole might win a distracted,

"That was delicious, honey," from a well meaning husband, but it wasn't enough.

In past generations, families could not have survived without "women's work." Spinning and weaving material for clothing and linens, manufacturing necessities such as candles, soap, and home medicines, canning and overseeing the garden and animals — a woman's tasks were backbreaking and vital.

But as society evolved from one in which items for family use were created at home to one that consumed articles manufactured elsewhere, the role of the housewife changed. By the fifties, her job description demanded maintaining high standards of cleanliness (from shiny floors to whiter than white underwear), cooking meals, and tending the children. And while it's easy to assume that labor saving devices like dishwashers, blenders, and automatic dryers cut down on the work load, that wasn't true. Studies done during the sixties showed that the time devoted to housework had increased over the previous forty years despite the explosion of automated household gadgets supposedly designed to make some jobs obsolete. The reason? Maintenance chores that took little time or attention earlier in the century grew to massive importance. Maintaining eat-off-the-floor standards, especially in a house full of kids and pets, can be a full-time job. Cooking from scratch, traveling from store to store in search of bargains, preparing homemade dog food, and sorting, folding, and ironing laundry filled the hours of every housewife's day and left her feeling drained and often irritable. She couldn't laugh when her husband, returning home to an immaculate house and well-scrubbed children, paid her by asking, "What do you do all day?"

It is not difficult to understand why, even in her own eyes, a housewife in the middle half of the twentieth century might have had difficulty in maintaining feelings of self-worth. Repeating the same chores, no matter how well you do them, can only remain a source of pride for so long.

Interestingly enough, psychologists and other "advice-givers" in the fifties, cautioned mothers of the time against "smothering" their children — giving them too much attention. Yet few, if any experts, suggested that work, even part-time, outside the home might release children from the grasp of overly controlling mothers or help women feel better about themselves.

But despite the experts' lack of enthusiasm, women continued to join the work force in growing numbers. Rising inflation and an expanding job market drew more and more women. While in the 1950s a majority of working women had no children under eighteen, by the 1960s the number of women having both kids and jobs continued to rise until, in 1972, for the first time, more mothers of school-age children were employed than were not.

At the same time that women were beginning to work outside the home, child care experts and society itself refused to recognize the facts. Pressure remained on women to bear the entire burden of raising children and keeping up the house. How could women help but feel frustrated?

The demands of motherhood amazed Erma. Exhaustion stalked her constantly. There weren't enough hours in the day. She never had time for herself and sagged under a kind of loneliness she had never known. Since no one discussed these feelings in public, Erma thought something was wrong with her, that she was the only woman in the world experiencing them. She thought she should be able to handle her life, but she wasn't doing a very good job, and no one seemed to understand.

Her solution was to bury herself in typical fifties housewifely pursuits. She crocheted Santa Claus doorknob covers, stuck contact paper on everything that didn't move, and decorated Bill's dinners with miniature roses sculpted from zucchini. It didn't help.

4

Birth of a Career

For a year after Betsy was born, Erma played doting mother and science teacher's wife. She had no plans to return to newspaper work, but when she was offered the opportunity to edit the *Dayton Shopping News*, she grabbed the chance. The little paper contained mostly ads, but once again, Erma vented her timely wit in a personal column. Motherhood filled one void, she realized, her writing another.

She branched out. As an advertising copywriter, Erma assumed a termite control account. For five years, she performed public relations duties as a consultant for four local YWCAs, writing press releases and publicizing their work. None of the paying positions pried more than a day's time from a week.

Although the doctor had claimed Erma would never conceive a child, she twice proved him wrong. In 1955, Andrew was born, followed by Matthew three years later.

In 1955, the Bombecks moved to Centerville, the city where Bill taught, and settled on a street bustling with growing families. Phil Donahue, his wife, and five children lived across the street. It was here that Erma began to change. For the first time, she met other women who were as frustrated as she was and who admitted it. As their kids raced up and down the streets on bicycles or played cops and robbers among the trees; the women talked. It came as a great relief to Erma that she wasn't on the verge of a nervous breakdown but was simply suffering from isolation and the normal wear and tear that kids inflict on their mothers. She was no different from anyone else. If anything, she was the typical housewife of the time, presenting a brave face, a relatively clean living room, and a recipe box crammed with Campbell's®Soup casseroles to the world

The Bombecks, a typical 1950s family.

while underneath she simmered with a kind of fiery resentment that terrified her. Learning she was not alone helped. She began to put life in perspective. She realized that the world wouldn't end if Andy left the house wearing a new tennis shoe on one foot and a dirty moccasin on the other. She wouldn't be asked to leave the United States if she fixed chicken twice in the same week. And Bill would survive without having his underwear ironed.

All this newfound wisdom demanded an outlet. Editing the *Dayton Shopping News* didn't provide it. Although she denies being ambitious, it was obvious Erma was thinking ahead when she thumbed through the local phone book and noticed that many Dayton newspaper editors lived in the surrounding suburbs. She guessed that if she happened to secure a column in the local paper, the editors would see it. Then, well, who knows. Maybe she'd be discovered. She laughed at the thought, and then, one day in 1964, Erma walked into the office of Ron Ginger, the editor of the local paper, the *Kettering-Oakwood Times*. "I'd like to do a column for you," she said. Simple honesty won the day. The editor fell for her charming intro and offered three dollars a week, and with a hand-shake—although neither she nor Ron Ginger realized it at the time—Erma Bombeck took a giant step on the road to fame and fortune.

At the beginning, "Zone 59" (the column's title referred to the Centerville area postal code) covered local happenings. The straightforward announcement of the South of Dayton YWCA's moving its daytime program outlined who, what, where, when, and why and was accompanied by Erma's inimitable light touch—"The YWCA program arrived in the South of Dayton area in 1956 just ahead of the crab grass . . ."

The columns profiled local characters or explained phenomenon only the home-grown could appreciate. Like the story about the gentleman who test-drove thirty-two miles of bus routes on snowy mornings to see for himself whether or not the schools should open that day. Or another mapping three miles of "spiritual" road, the route north of Centerville that boasted seven churches.

As Erma grew more comfortable with the format, her now trademark writing style began to surface. "Being named to Centerville's Coed Drill team seems to be the biggest thing that can happen to a girl," she wrote. "A Centerville high school girl, that is. She's not too thin, too tall, too short or too heavy, who has a flare for the dance and can march three miles without fainting. And she doesn't mind burying her bangs and teased hair under a stewardess hat."

Her potshots at the homemaker's lot began to surface in column openings like this: "Next to the virus and pregnancy nausea, no other disease hits the homemaker as hard as mid-winter 'Stir-phobia.'

"It's brought about by too much snow, too many children indoors and too little precious time to devote to oneself. The symptoms are short temper, floor pacing and occasionally throwing yourself under a garbage truck to start a conversation."

Eventually Erma dropped the localization and began to write columns with wider appeal. An early one publicized "Letters I never mailed" and included the following:

Dear Mr. Exterminator:

First let me assure you that not for one minute do I believe every commercial I see on television. When you showed ants screaming hysterically, clutching their throats and eventually falling dead while a tombstone and large flower arose out of their chest, I knew this was exaggerated to get me to buy your product.

However, I don't feel I'm unreasonable to expect just one of our ants to stagger or cough however inaudibly.

After distributing your product throughout, I observed them at some length and they are gobbling up

47

the poison like Swedish meat balls at an 11 P.M. dinner party. I can assure you their numbers have not decreased. They are assembled in an orderly fashion about the table at 8 A.M., high noon and 6 P.M. with irritating timing. I fully expect them to ask for "doggie bags" to take away what they can't eat under the table.

Would you please be so kind as to refund the $1.69 I spent on your product. I would suggest you and your scientist friends skip lunch and get back to the drawing boards.

Sincerely, Incensed Housewife.

For over a year and a half, Erma's weekly contributions to the *Kettering-Oakwood Times* discussed the life of the town less and less. Instead, Erma poured out the pent-up emotions that shadowed her life. The words might have been jotted in a diary, they were so personal. "I didn't care if anyone read it or liked it or bought it," she says. "I needed an outlet for my own feelings, for my own survival."

The words spilled out like a gushing waterfall. The columns were easy to write, and Erma could hardly wait for each week to roll around so she could attack the next topic she wanted to get off her chest. Writing was fun, too—like doodling with a typewriter, Erma says.

From the beginning, professionalism marked Erma's work. She instinctively knew what good column writing entailed. Hook 'em with the lead. Hold 'em with laughter. Exit with a quip they won't forget.

"Zone 59" became a humor column. The writing wasn't profound. The columns didn't move people like her later writings would, but they gave women the chance to laugh at themselves and their lives in a way no one else had ever done.

Having been trained in a newsroom where dozens of people milled about and typewriters chattered and chimed, Erma could write despite the chaos around her. She turned out her columns in a cramped bedroom, the typewriter balanced on a plank suspended between a couple of cinderblocks. The children taunted and teased each other, and through the closed doors the noise reached her, but Erma blocked it out.

The column had run for some time in the *Kettering-Oakwood Times* when Glenn Thompson, the *Dayton Journal-Herald*'s editor, spotted her work. Thompson offered to up her pay and her work load—$50 a week for two columns to run under her byline—if she

The talented Bombeck crew in the 1950s.

would return to her old stomping ground. Erma could not imagine anything she wanted to do more. Fifteen years before she had been mixing paste, and now her old paper had invited her back as a columnist. What better treat could possibly lie in store?

What happened next still astounds Erma. Thompson sent a few of her columns to the Newsday Newspaper Syndicate and suggested they might be interested in syndicating Erma nationally. They were. Three weeks after her first column appeared in the *Dayton Journal-Herald,* Erma signed a short-term contract with Newsday. Thirty-eight papers were buying her 400–500 word columns by the end of the first year. Five years later "At Wit's End" was a staple in 500.

Syndication gives writers and cartoonists the opportunity to appear in hundreds of newspapers. Syndicates market their work for them by distributing editorial cartoons, puzzles, games, single articles, and book excerpts to newspapers all over the country. It would be a full-time job for writers and artists to meet every newspaper editor in the country, sell the product, and work out

Erma celebrates the holiday one year with the staff of the *Dayton Journal-Herald.*

financial arrangements. Instead, the artists put themselves in the hands of newspaper syndicates. Writers and cartoonists produce, and the syndicates sell, promote, and distribute the product. They also receive a percentage of the writer/cartoonist's salary. The salary depends on the size of the newspaper. The bigger the paper, the more money it pays. A newspaper with half a million in circulation might pay $200 a week while a country weekly could get the same column for $3.

In 1988, Erma moved her column to Universal Press Syndicate. Over the years, she had been with a number of others. It's like deciding where to shop, Erma says. A lot of stores offer the same merchandise, but some display the items better or will take returns without a receipt. Syndicates vary in the number of features they take on; the number of new features launched each year; the size and quality of their sales staff; and the degree of aggressiveness with which they merchandise their contributors.

Universal Press Syndicate currently distributes Erma's columns to more than 700 newspapers. UPS, located in Kansas City, Missouri, is the largest independent syndicate in the country and the third or fourth largest of all syndicates. The company offers seventy-five features including comics such as "Doonsbury," "Herman," "The Far Side," and "Ziggy." Besides Erma, the company syndicates Abigail Van Buren, better known as "Dear Abby," and a number of respected political writers.

Since newspapers have only a limited amount of space, they may cancel a feature that isn't drawing or holding readers and substitute another. That's why the syndicate's sales staff is so important. They need to understand and appreciate the features they are marketing, as well as the goals of potential newspaper clients.

Erma looks for a company that believes in her and operates an aggressive sales force. She also likes to work for nice people. She doesn't make demands, but she expects a personal approach from an editor she respects and trusts.

Syndicates receive up to 10,000 submissions a year from would-be columnists and cartoonists. Most syndicates take on a few new writers/artists each year. Universal Press Syndicate has launched a number of unknowns who have become household names. Cathy Guisewite, who produces the successful cartoon feature "Cathy," sent samples of her work "over the transom" (without being asked). The editors at Universal liked her work so much that they mailed her a contract the same day! Every business needs new blood and new ideas, and no one knows who will be the next Erma Bombeck. Syndicates' willingness to seek out and support writers pressures columnists like Erma Bombeck. If her work ever grows stale, no matter how long she's been on board, she will disappear. Syndicates and newspapers often renew their contracts every thirty days. They can drop columns at any time. Even a writer like Erma, who would seem secure at the top, cannot afford to slack off.

In a way, Erma enjoys the pressure. It's a form of discipline that keeps her doing her best no matter how she feels on a particular day. In the twenty-five years Erma has been writing her column, she has missed only one deadline. A tropical disease knocked her out of commission for a day.

Every Monday Erma sends three columns to Kansas City. From there they are distributed to hundreds of newspapers. She writes two weeks in advance. Occasionally she gets caught. When the National Football League was considering canceling the Super Bowl, Erma worried. She had submitted a column relating to the event. If it had been canceled, the column wouldn't have made much sense.

Most people would be surprised to learn that after twenty-five years, Erma still works with an editor. She and Alan McDermott, her Universal Press editor, may spend as long as four hours in debating the finer points of one week's three 450-word columns. Erma listens carefully to her editor's ideas and input, but she knows what she wants, what her readers like, and what works, and she usually gets it.

There are more than 300 syndicates in the country but only seven or eight important ones. It's tough to break into a syndicate today, probably tougher than it was when Erma started because there is relatively little syndicated work purchased by newspapers. The local papers will buy only what they cannot provide themselves. In addition, it's hard to come up with an original, timely idea.

Erma is certain that timing played a vital role in the instant success of her column. Women were more ready for what she had to say than anyone imagined. They were tired of the image of perfection that society had thrust on them. They were prepared to show the world their shortcomings and ask for a little sympathy. Not just in Kettering, Ohio, but obviously in cities, towns, and hamlets across the country, they were anxious to listen to the words of a woman who was one of them.

Her humor was pure identification. It never put down the women it amused. Women could laugh at themselves because Erma, who shared their lives, stood first in line. She let them know that the laughter was necessary to their survival, that some things in life were serious, but housework wasn't one of them.

Sitting in Centerville, typing her brains out, Erma was content. This was fun. But despite the unprecedented spread of her columns across the country, she had no idea whether people were reading her words or using them to line their birdcages.

As more newspapers signed her on, though, Erma was asked to lecture in the new cities. The thousands of women (and a surprising number of men) who turned out to hear her speak, applauding her every poke at their lives, thrilled and overwhelmed her. Their laughter rolled in great waves through the auditorium and confirmed that at long last they had found someone who understood them.

At first, Erma delighted in the trips, in meeting her fans who affirmed her life and work. Later, she grew tired of the endless series of hotel rooms and of being away from her family. She eventually left the speakers' circuit. But in 1966, it was new and exciting, and she enjoyed every minute.

5

Erma's Fame Grows

As the number of newspapers that carried Erma's column grew, new opportunities opened up for her. Doubleday suggested publishing a compilation of a number of her columns. Erma, like most first-time authors, assumed the book's publication meant riches and fame. She imagined dozens of copies prominently displayed in bookstore windows from New York to Los Angeles. Her relatives would surely clog phone lines ordering staggering numbers of copies. Major television networks would scramble for the opportunity to interview the latest star on the literary scene. Erma painted herself a glorious picture. Unfortunately, it didn't happen. Her relatives didn't stampede the stores, and neither, for a long time, did anyone else. Dressed in her best, she perched behind card tables set up in bookstores so she could autograph *At Wit's End*—only to find she was lucky if anyone else showed up. The success she imagined the first book would bring seemed an illusion. Erma suffered a big letdown. She felt very discouraged. But once the initial disappointment passed, her natural optimism kicked in.

Erma understood that for every person who accepted a Pulitzer Prize or an Academy Award, hundreds stood empty-handed. They might be just as worthy. But maybe the competition was just too stiff. Maybe the sentimental favorite took the honors. Maybe the others hadn't yet paid their dues. She thought that the screenwriter now clutching the statue, thanking everyone who'd known him from the moment he was born, had undoubtedly lived through years when his talents had gone unrewarded. "Success," said Erma firmly, "is outliving your failures." She planned to do just that.

In fact, the book, released in 1967, sold moderately well, about as expected for a first-time author just beginning to gain recognition through her triweekly humorous commentaries.

Erma, a complete novice in the book world, was also disappointed to learn that publishing companies don't invest huge sums of money in first-time authors even if they are syndicated three times a week in newspapers around the country. They don't send them on extended promotional tours, and they make no effort to get them on important television talk shows where a single appearance can generate thousands of sales. These are saved for the big guns— which of course Erma became one day. But back in 1967, she jokes, she appeared on radio programs with Roy Rogers' horse and signed autographs in laundromats.

But wherever Erma spoke, listeners couldn't whip their money out fast enough. Audiences related to her. She was no glamour queen. Her words lacked the practiced polish of professional politicians. But there was something about Erma Bombeck. There wasn't a fake bone in her body. She was a real housewife—not a sanitized Hollywood version whose babies never spit up, whose dogs always sat up, and whose families rarely split up. Erma spent her days hauling kids from dentist to dance lessons and her nights searching for socks the dryer ate. Her ordinariness, her candor, her self-deprecating humor fed a public bored with glamorized images. Erma reflected her audiences. They fell in love with her. And they bought her book.

Even young people, who hardly picked up a newspaper and so

were unfamiliar with Erma's columns, dove into the book *At Wit's End*. They related to the family setting and the way Erma (Mom) reacted. She was just like their mothers. Sometimes the parents looked foolish, and the kids even won a few rounds. The book depicted their lives as honestly as anything they had probably seen. It wasn't a comic book, but it made them laugh. When the teacher asked for a book report, they'd choose Erma's book. Lots of kids memorized Erma's satiric slices of family life for speech competitions. Since little humor was being written for young people, Erma's book filled a void. Through the years and the cascade of books that Erma has published, kids continue to thank her for helping them understand their families (especially their mothers) better.

Anyone who listens to Erma Bombeck toss out jokes on television today might have difficulty imagining how hard it was for her to stand up in front of people and speak. She wasn't trained as an actress or comedian. She had studied English, psychology, and philosophy. Just because you can "write funny" doesn't mean you can "act funny." Telling amusing stories with a degree of professionalism requires more than good material. One-liners that read well may leave great puddles of "dead air" when spoken. But Erma was a quick study. She listened when her audiences laughed. She noted blank stares and raised eyebrows that indicated she'd lost them. And she rarely made the mistake twice.

When Erma began to travel in support of her books, she wrote out her speeches, but never read them. Instead, she printed reminders on 3" x 5" cards. Since she primarily shared anecdotes, just a word or two launched each story. And while she has never claimed to be a comedian, her timing improved with experience. After years of facing audiences, Erma grew more comfortable with her role. But at the beginning, doubts shadowed her. She would stand off-stage in an auditorium swollen with a thousand eager fans and wonder how she had gotten herself into this mess. Her heart thundered so loudly she feared it would overpower her words. Waves of self-doubt washed over her. Then she'd take a deep breath and pull herself together. She'd greet her audience with a smile and plunge in. Knowing that the people who'd come to listen didn't expect her to be anything but herself helped. And once the first laugh bounded across the footlights, she'd feel fine. Eventually, as Erma made more and more live appearances, she grew more confident. But she never lost the magic formula that drew people to her in the first place—she stayed simply Erma.

A Doubleday sales representative named Aaron Priest met Erma in Dallas on one of her promotional jaunts. Salespeople from publishing houses are responsible for pushing all the books in their company's yearly line. To do a good job, they need to be convinced that the books they are selling are entertaining, well written, or just plain "hot." But they also need to be good listeners. When bookstore owners tell them that a particular book is generating a firestorm of interest, good salespeople take notice.

In 1967, as Aaron Priest toured the stores in his territory, he began to hear the same story from owners. He'd ask them how the company's "big book" (the most "important" or highly prized author's new release) was doing, and they would demand more copies of *At Wit's End*. Everywhere he went, the bookstore owners talked about the women who stood laughing in the aisles as they thumbed through the book and who just plain loved Erma's writing. Books flew out of the stores.

Priest contacted the publishing company in New York and urged them to push the book. They ignored his advice. The company evidently didn't share Priest's excitement or belief in Erma. Were they wrong! Twenty-five years after publication, she continues to receive royalties of about $16,000 a year from *At Wit's End*. She can't remember what she was paid for the original rights to the book, but she does recall that the paperback rights sold for the grand sum of $750.

She also remembers kneeling on the floor of the bathroom in Centerville, laying a piece of carpet around the toilet, when she heard Arthur Godfrey, a well-known talk-show host of the time, discussing *At Wit's End* on his show: He sarcastically noted that this author who portrayed herself as "just a housewife" probably lived luxuriously in a New York City penthouse. Erma wrote to him pointing out his mistake and ended up as a regular guest on his program.

Aaron Priest remained with Doubleday as Erma published two more books. One day she received a card from him. He had left Doubleday. He mentioned that if she ever had an idea for a book and needed an agent or someone to bounce her thoughts off, just give him a call. Maybe she'd like him to act as her agent. Until that point, Erma had worked without an agent. In light of her later success, the amount of money she undoubtedly lost by signing contracts on her own can hardly be called catastrophic, but like most artists, she had little interest and less knowledge of the fine art of negotiation. Having her books published and receiving a small sum as an acknowledgment of the creative work involved seemed reward enough.

But the world of publishing is not a simple one. Publishers seek to earn as much as possible for the services they provide. Writers expect a living wage for their work. Negotiating a contract from which both author and publishing company benefit is like walking barefoot in a cow pasture. Everyone involved had better pay close attention.

Generally writers are not knowledgeable enough about publishing to secure the best deals for themselves. That's why they hire agents. Agents play matchmaker between writers and publishing companies. They know the kinds of books each publishing company wants. Sometimes agents act as collaborators in the early stages of writing. Knowledgeable about the latest trends in the industry, they may work with authors to help define the audience for a book. Depending on the agency, agents can screen speaking or writing requests and help with book promotion. But their most important contribution usually lies in negotiating contracts that benefit their clients. A good agent attempts to retain not only the "standard" rights assumed to belong the author, but also television or movie rights with massive financial potential.

For her first three books, Erma handled the details herself, but when she came up with the idea for the fourth, she tapped one of her strongest supporters, Aaron Priest. Priest was delighted to take on Erma as a client. He was convinced she was going to be one of the most successful writers in the country. He was also convinced that no one was doing a very good job of supporting this blossoming talent.

The idea Erma shared with Aaron in a phone call revolved around paralleling the settlement of the suburbs with the settlement of the American West. He asked her to send him an outline or a few pages of the book. She told him she would, but also mentioned her jammed schedule. She didn't want to write the book immediately. She didn't have time. "It's just an idea," she insisted. "Don't do anything with it."

He called her two weeks later and said, "My God, Erma, this has got to be worth six figures." She snapped back, "Don't tell my husband!" But she found time to write the book.

Aaron was amazed how little money Erma had made on previous books. "If anyone has paid their dues, it's Erma," he says.

Two weeks after receiving the outline, he'd sold *The Grass Is Always Greener Over the Septic Tank* to McGraw-Hill. Doubleday wasn't willing to meet the price he demanded.

Aaron brought not only his faith in Erma to the deals he made for her but also his expertise. When he sold *The Grass is Always Greener Over the Septic Tank,* he had been off his salesman's route for only eighteen months. He knew how to market Erma Bombeck. The proof came when she hit the bestseller lists for the first time in her career. The hardcover edition eventually sold more than

500,000 copies and the paperback over three million in the United States alone.

But despite her columns' reach and the monumental sales her books began rolling up, it took a long time for real success to find Erma Bombeck. She probably wasn't flashy enough. Her face never peered out from supermarket tabloids. She couldn't seem to cook up a scandal that would get people talking. For years, she could amble through airports without being recognized or finish dinner in a restaurant without even one diner asking for an autograph. But even when, eventually, she stepped into the glaring light of fame, she didn't change. People who "knew her when" say she's the same person she was back in Dayton. Erma discovered, though, that people around her changed. Once she was walking in Dayton, and she saw someone she had gone to school with. She waved, then called to the woman who had almost passed by. "Hey, don't you know who I am? I haven't seen you in so many years. Have I changed so much?" The woman stopped and sniffed. "Well, I didn't think you'd remember me." The icy tone cut Erma. But worse was the recognition that whether she had changed or not, some people assumed she had. And the change, they thought, could not possibly be for the better. Some people believe that the famous automatically forget where they came from, ignore their old friends, and care nothing for the life they left behind. Maybe that's true for some people, but not for Erma. It was difficult for her to accept the cold shoulder from former acquaintances. She knew being famous, even wealthy, hadn't changed her, but it was difficult to convey this fact to other people who believe that fame brings with it a self-centeredness that leaves little room for old relationships. It saddened Erma that people who knew her in the past felt uncomfortable around her, but she realized it was up to her to put them at ease, to reassure them that no matter how famous she became and no matter how much money she made, she still thought of herself as little Erma Fiste of Dayton, Ohio.

61

Erma found a comfortable if sometimes frantic pattern evolving as she continued to turn out newspaper columns and books. In 1969, she was asked to provide a monthly column—"Up the Wall"—for *Good Housekeeping* magazine, a service she continued for six years. Periodically she wrote for other magazines, including *Reader's Digest, Family Circle, Redbook, McCall's,* and even *Teen.* In 1971, her second book, *Just Wait Till You Have Children of Your Own,* coauthored by Bil Keane, originator of the popular "Family Circus" cartoons, hit the bookstores.

Several years before, the Bombecks had moved their brood to a thirty-acre farm in idyllic Bellbrook, Ohio. The pastoral setting proved relaxing but at the same time taxing since the children felt a farm should be populated with lots of animals. Erma traveled around the country from the Ohio home base until one day she gave a speech in Phoenix. The midwestern native fell hard for the desert—the stunning sunsets, the craggy mountains, and the oddly twisted cactus dotting the landscape. Besides, the audience that night fell in love with her. That sealed it. Not long afterwards, the Bombeck family traded the cows' mournful moos for the coyotes' eerie cries and resettled in Arizona.

Bill found a job as a high school principal, and Erma continued her hectic pace, attempting to balance marriage, motherhood, and a work schedule guaranteed to land most people in bed with chronic exhaustion. At one point, she complained about her limited life-style, calling herself "one-dimensional" and a "loner." It seemed to Erma that all she did was work. She had no time to make friends and missed the lively companionship of her Ohio neighbors.

I Lost Everything in the Post-Natal Depression, Erma's next book, released in 1974, helped endear the writer to thousands of new mothers across the country. The book took a hard look at the thankless tasks of new motherhood, the same ones Erma had cried over some years before. She hoped with this book to ease the burden of new moms by helping them to spot the humor in their situations.

As Erma's books became more popular, she traveled more and more to promote them. Months before a book is released, marketing plans are drawn up. Every move is calculated with an eye toward selling as many copies as possible in the shortest period of time. The public loses interest very quickly. For many years, Erma trekked around the country promoting her current book for as long as ten weeks at a time, parading through cities and towns from one end of the United States to the other. She claims that by the end of one tour she was so exhausted that she forgot who she was and autographed several dozen books with another author's name!

While Erma loved writing and enjoyed her growing popularity with readers, each new book, article, or trip to some faraway city to speak made her feel more isolated. Success was forcing her to abandon a normal life. She'd forgotten how to relax and have fun. If she wasn't working, she grew restless. Bill worried about her health. Finally, she took a hard look and decided something had to go. The something was lecturing, which, although it enabled her to interact with her fans, demanded a heavy price. The traveling sapped her energy. It took days to recover from the trips. And Erma, who had never grown bored churning out her columns, began to tire of hearing herself speak. She struggled to maintain the vitality and enthusiasm that made her a successful speaker in the first place. Her children were growing up. The balancing act between the two top priorities in her life—work and family—had begun to tilt too far to the former.

Freedom from lecturing provided her with more time to be the mother and wife she wanted to be, but she never backed off her commitment to writing. Her first three books had sold well, but with the fourth, *The Grass Is Always Greener Over the Septic Tank*, published in 1976, Erma hit the big time. Her lighthearted look at suburban living spent more than ten months on the best-seller lists and sold over half a million copies. As Erma told her agent, "I think I'm finally starting to figure out how to do this."

6

A Growing Career and Political Involvement

Soon after *The Grass Is Always Greener Over the Septic Tank* hit the best-seller lists, Erma received a call from producer Bob Shanks, who was putting together a new television show for ABC. NBC's *Today* show had been sounding the public's wake-up call since 1952, but according to critics of the time, it had grown predictable and dull. Yet with no programming to challenge it, *Today* continued to pull a sizable audience.

Bob Shanks took up the challenge. With *Good Morning America*, he hoped to create a program that informed and entertained at the same time, one that provided women with advice and ideas on how to run their homes.

Before talking to Erma, Shanks had already assembled a large and impressive cast, including David Hartman (who had starred in a TV western called *Lucas Tanner*), Nancy Dussault (a television actress), Jack Anderson (a syndicated political newspaper columnist), Rona Barrett (her beat was Hollywood), Jonathan Winters (a roly-poly comedian), and Geraldo Rivera. Erma's response?

The original *Good Morning America* family.

"I can't imagine all those people in the same country let alone on the same show. I think you're out of your mind."

While Shanks seemed to agree with Erma's assessment regarding his state of mind, he was convinced that the concept would work, and he wanted her to be a part of it. He asked her to do two- or three-minute humorous "bits" and promised that her portions of the program would be filmed in Phoenix.

She had already appeared on some of the well-known talk shows, including the *Tonight Show* and *Donahue*, promoting *The Grass Is Always Greener Over the Septic Tank,* and she felt comfortable on television. The money was great, and she wouldn't have to leave the family. She said, "Yes."

Her decision proved a good one. *Good Morning America* hit the air in 1975 with easygoing David Hartman heading up the odd mix of characters Bob Shanks had harnessed. The program's set echoed a suburban home complete with a cozy living room and a kitchen where Julia Child could share recipes and Mary Ellen Pinkham offer household hints to viewers. *Today*, on the other hand, installed its anchors behind a horseshoe-shaped desk backed by a backdrop of the Manhattan skyline. Where David Hartman resembled an easygoing family doctor, Tom Brokaw and Jane Pauley, the *Today* anchors, were at the time considered efficient, distant, and lacking any real warmth. Willard Scott, the *Today* show's weatherman, got points for his country-boy humor, but the big brother of morning shows seemed to take itself very seriously. Although *Good Morning America* opened with the news, it quickly left the bad stuff behind and drew viewers with celebrity interviews and information on how to improve their lives.

Five years would pass, however, before *Good Morning America* surpassed the *Today* show in the ratings. In 1980, for the first time, *Good Morning America* topped its morning competition (including the third place *Morning* on CBS) for thirty-three weeks straight. The shows continued to seesaw in popularity right through the eighties.

Erma's stint on *Good Morning America* lasted eleven years. What began as two or three minutes of her zany twist on life evolved into longer interviews with celebrities, including Zsa Zsa Gabor (whom she interviewed in Zsa Zsa's king-size bed) and comedienne Phyllis Diller.

But regardless of how famous or important her interviewee, Erma never played the interrogator. Talking with her was like chatting with a friend. Employing a down-home, relaxed style, Erma posed the kinds of questions fans were dying to have answered. Movie stars felt secure, comfortable, and unafraid with Erma. Unlike an investigative reporter whose job it is to dig up all the information, good and bad, on the person she is researching, Erma tried only to unmask the human and humorous side of people.

Most celebrities responded well to her. Some, like Barbara Mandrell, enjoyed turning the tables. One night, during a concert in Indiana, Mandrell said, "Erma Bombeck is in the audience. She thinks this is such a fun, easy business. Hey, Erma, come on up here and sing." Despite the fact that Erma knew about as much about country music as she did about nuclear medicine, she gave it her best, much to the amusement and joy of the audience.

Interviews involved traveling to various locations throughout the country to visit not only celebrities, but also ordinary people who lived quirky lives.

Erma loved interviewing people and was continually astonished by what they revealed to her. She'd pull up in front of someone's home, clip a microphone on their undershirt, and blurt out questions which, much to her amazement they would answer without a shred of embarrassment. "They'd tell me anything," she said with a laugh.

One of her favorite interviews was with a woman named Roy Rogers. Rogers, in her late seventies, was famous for nothing more than reading. Erma couldn't believe they were flying a crew all the way to Minnesota to interview a woman who read.

Erma was wired with a microphone so she could start the interview as soon as she got out of the car. As she drew up to a rundown old house, she spotted Rogers, dressed in jeans, rolling a cigarette and leaning against an enormous motorcycle.

The house was falling apart. Erma couldn't figure out how the woman survived in winter. But in the kitchen stood a straight-back chair and a rickety table topped with a gooseneck lamp. Roy Rogers

Barbara Mandrell and Erma ready to go to bat during the 1988 Celebrity Softball classic.

would sit and twine her feet around the legs of that chair and pore over everything from Shakespeare to Steinbeck.

When Rogers discovered that Erma had been an English major, she exclaimed, "Thank God you can talk about books." The discussion that followed charmed not only Erma, but also millions of *Good Morning America* viewers.

Erma thrived with the supportive crew and loosely styled *Good Morning America* interviews. But eventually she grew tired of the travel, which carved ten days from each month. She decided to quit. It was hard to give up the show because she prized the job and adored the people she worked with. But she was exhausted. For more than a decade, in addition to two *Good Morning America* pieces a week, she had continued her column, "At Wit's End,"

Being a TV star isn't always fun.

written more books, produced a television show, and, with Bill, managed to raise her children. Charlie Gibson, who had joined *Good Morning America*, arrived at the studio on her last day and said, "I just had to come in and see for myself. I've never seen anyone turn their back and walk away from this business." Other people probably wondered too, wondered if there was some undisclosed reason Erma was leaving. But she insists she was ready to go, ready to return to a more normal existence, and she has never regretted leaving.

In 1978, Erma was appointed to the President's National Advisory Committee for Women. The committee had originally been launched by President Franklin D. Roosevelt, who sought input from women representing every aspect of American political, ethnic, and religious life. He asked this group to act as his eyes and ears in the country, relaying to him women's thoughts and ideas as they might impact American life.

Every president since Franklin D. Roosevelt until Ronald Reagan continued the committee, and under Jimmy Carter, Erma joined a distinguished group of forty women, including Linda Robb (the daughter of President Lyndon B. Johnson), Ann Richards (the first female commissioner in Travis County, Texas, and later the governor of Texas), and Bella Abzug (congresswoman from New York), who kept their fingers on the pulse of women in America. They periodically met with the president to outline issues important to women and discuss ways Congress might address the needs of women.

Erma believed that over the three and a half years she attended meetings, President Carter listened and took their ideas and thoughts seriously.

Although Erma appreciated being asked to join the commission, she never considered herself a political activist. In fact, she'd never been particularly interested in politics. But one issue forced her into the political arena. It was the Equal Rights Amendment.

In 1972, Congress approved a constitutional amendment guaranteeing equal rights for women. The amendment stated: "Equality of rights under the law shall not be denied or abridged by the United States or any state on account of sex," and "that Congress shall have the power to enforce by appropriate legislation, the provisions of this article."

According to the Constitution, amendments, once approved by Congress, must be ratified by three-fourths of the states within seven years before becoming law.

Within a year of its Senate approval, the ERA was ratified by thirty states. Polls showed that Americans favored the amendment by a large majority, but after the first burst of enthusiastic support, the ERA suddenly became the most divisive issue of the time.

The early 1970s was a time of confused and shifting values

Erma was one of forty women chosen to represent America's female voice on the National Advisory Committee for Women.

especially when it came to women's roles. The National Organization for Women (NOW) spoke for the feminist viewpoint, which, while claiming to represent the voice of all women, seemed to many to denigrate the value of housewives and mothers while elevating women who worked outside the home to near sainthood. To counter the strident voice of feminism, religious groups formed what was to become a forceful constituency among women who felt forgotten in the face of increasing demands for "equal pay for equal work." Conservative political and religious organizations rallied against the ERA, railing against the possibility that passage might mean there would be no more separate toilet facilities for men and women and that women would be required, under the ERA, to serve in combat positions in the military. Neither of these scenarios or any of the others raised by the anti-ERA constituency would have automatically taken effect if the ERA passed. But the remotest possibility that they could come about, coupled with a liberal-minded Supreme Court, ignited passionate resistance to the amendment.

It surprised a lot of people when Erma Bombeck, voice of the American housewife, came out in support of the ERA. But Erma saw no conflict. She couldn't understand why anyone would object to equality for women. Discrimination of any kind had always angered her. How could women accept being left out of the Constitution of the United States?

Her staunch support of the amendment did not, however, include its feminist leaders, whom she felt were on the wrong track. She sensed they were waging a war using housewives as the battleground. Feminists proclaimed that women had choices. They could be anything they wanted to be except housewives. Housewives symbolized all that was wrong in American women. They were, in the view of feminists, tied to their kitchens under the thumb of dictatorial mates whose irrational demands turned the women into unthinking slaves. Leaders of the women's movement claimed housewives were depressed, neurotic, and unfulfilled. Erma agreed that sometimes women did experience these feelings. But having them didn't make their lives meaningless or imply that being a housewife was any less worthwhile than working as a secretary or, for that matter, president of a company. And as she got closer to the leadership, Erma discovered that housewives were simply not wanted as participants in the movement. She believed in true equality, that no matter how you spend your life, you deserve recognition and acceptance and that the contribution you make to society by caring for your family should be considered equal to that made by anyone working at a job with regulated hours and pay. If, Erma thought, housewives' lives were at the center of the battle, why not enlist their help? Who better to spread the word about inequities than the women who were suffering them? Instead, the movement denied them a role. Housewives, in turn, thought the leadership misunderstood them entirely.

Erma began an odyssey across the country under the auspices of ERA America, an organization whose only goal was to get the ERA passed. Erma never declared herself a feminist, although she has always supported some, but not all, of their goals. (She opposes abortion, for instance.) But Erma believed that when the laws of the land were written, women should have been included, and she spent two years of her life fighting to make it happen.

She traveled to almost every state where the battle for the ERA raged, but her political views never crept into her writing. By this time she had published six books of humor. In 1978, the paperback rights to *If Life Is a Bowl of Cherries, What Am I Doing in the Pits?* had sold for $1 million. Her most recent effort, *Aunt Erma's Cope Book,* had received a near-record advance printing of 700,000 hardcover copies. Her column had spread to 900 newspapers, and due to her *Good Morning America* appearances, millions of people recognized her face. Everywhere and always, Erma was celebrated as a humorist. What would people think about her tackling a constitutional amendment? She refused to worry, believing her readers and fans would accept her right to speak out on an important issue in which she believed.

Where others used political rhetoric in an attempt to force people to change, Erma relied, as always, on her wit. But she got the point across. Everyone who listened knew where Erma Bombeck stood. Occasionally, a fan would approach her before a speech, take her arm, and say, "I hope you're not going to disappoint me, Erma," and she would reply, "I hope I'm not." She felt a responsibility to her readers but more of a responsibility to a vital change she believed would impact women's lives in this country forever.

Erma and Liz Carpenter chat during a break in Erma's campaign for the Equal Rights Amendment.

Her fans were not disappointed in her. In fact, they rallied behind her, and she takes credit for changing some opinions. Women called her a "voice of sanity." When they heard that Erma was behind the amendment, they asked why. Once they understood, many joined her.

Not everyone supported her stance. An official in a southern state said she should be home having babies. A Salt Lake City bookstore removed her books from the window. She shrugged off insults and abuse hurled from the mouths of people who wanted nothing but to maintain things as they were, who were afraid that any change meant a change for the worse.

As she stood before crowds where insults rained down as often as applause, Erma developed a lasting respect for courageous activists who speak out no matter what the consequences. And while she felt a bit bruised and battered by it all, she relished her role. When asked by a reporter why she poured so much time and effort into the ERA, Erma replied, "I'm doing it for my kids. It will be important to them. It's also a great feeling to be a part of history. I wish that they could put this on my tombstone: She got Missouri for the ERA."

Unfortunately, despite an extension of three years, time ran out and the ERA failed. It was one of the biggest disappointments of Erma Bombeck's life.

7

Success and Failure

With the success of Erma's spots on *Good Morning America*, all kinds of offers poured in. One was to adapt *The Grass Is Always Greener Over the Septic Tank* for a television movie, which, if successful, might lead to a permanent sitcom slot. On October 25, 1978, the TV movie starring Carol Burnett and Charles Grodin aired on CBS. Critics hated it. One wrote in *Time* magazine, "Let's hope that someone at CBS had the good sense to mow *Grass* down at this early stage."

A year later, ABC, not in the least deterred by *Grass's* dismal showing, gave Erma a licensing fee to develop a situation comedy. She thought up a concept and pitched it to Marcy Carsey and Tom Werner (who have since produced a number of television hits including *The Cosby Show*). They liked it. Erma had never written a script and knew nothing about creating a television series, but she agreed to do some of the writing.

Erma drew the television family from her own life. The show looked at an ordinary, though slightly manic family from—guess where?—Dayton, Ohio. Erma fought to make the mother of the family, Maggie, believable. She didn't want Maggie outfitted in the latest fashion, sporting a hairstyle that only the Queen of England could afford. Maggie and her family (including a son who was never seen since he'd entered the bathroom when he hit puberty), as Erma envisioned them, were down-to-earth, no-frills types who struggled with everyday problems and often lost. Erma insisted women were tired of seeing themselves portrayed as smiling plastic dolls who managed to cook six-course gourmet dinners, sew prom dresses for five daughters, and solve their husbands' paycheck woes all in thirty minutes with time out for commercials.

Everyone who needed to loved the pilot for *Maggie*, and the team received the go-ahead to produce a number of episodes. At this point, the executive producer announced that another pilot he had made was also being picked up. Unable to handle two new series, he dropped out. Erma was promoted to executive producer, something she knew even less about than writing television scripts. She had no clue what she was to do, but she realized with a sinking heart that several dozen people were depending on her. Not only had the studio invested a lot of money in her concept, but if she refused, everyone from the actors to the camera people, lighting technicians, and costume designers would lose their jobs. How could she say no?

She rented an apartment in Los Angeles. Awakening at 5:00 A.M., she'd dash off a column before climbing into a rented Toyota, race to Studio City by 9:00 A.M., work on scripts, oversee run-throughs, dress rehearsals, and editing until 9:00 P.M., fall into bed, wake up, and do it all again. On Friday nights, she would turn in the car at the Burbank airport and fly home to Bill and the kids, then boomerang back to L.A. again. She followed this routine for four months.

The network ordered thirteen episodes. She hired writers but wrote five of the first eight scripts herself. The show, starring Miriam Flynn in the title role, hung on for eight weeks before it was canceled. Much to Erma's amazement, although the show died, the studio directors had no complaints. They asked her to develop another series. Erma turned them down flat. There was no way she could have kept up the crazy schedule any longer. She was exhausted. But she wasn't emotionally distraught over what the press insisted on calling a failure.

Erma's expectations are never very high, but she believes that if you don't try, you can't possibly succeed. She agreed to get into the TV production business because she thought it would be fun. She enjoys challenges and wanted to try something new. But she refuses to attach her ego to projects. She doesn't place life and death importance on anything outside of her family. If you knocked a priceless piece of china (assuming she had one) off Erma's shelf, she'd likely utter, "That's too bad," on the way to get the broom. That would be the end of it.

When *Maggie* was canceled, Erma felt bad for all the people involved, but she couldn't have kept up the pace she'd run during those four months anyway. Some members of the press asked her how she felt about being a failure. Erma replied, "You have the words wrong. I failed at something; I'm not a failure." She admitted failing at something every day. She'd had columns that didn't quite come off and had appeared on talk shows where she felt she'd embarrassed herself. But she shrugged the feelings off and thought about tomorrow. She never let it eat into her or let her ego get in the way of her work. She knew going in to *Maggie* that the odds of success were small. Twenty-three new shows debuted that year. Erma wasn't the only one whose concept bombed. She had plenty of company. One critic, after sitting through previews of every new show, pegged 1981 as "the worst season in boob-tube history." Almost none of the shows launched in the fall of 1981 surfaced the next season.

But to Erma, the experience was far from a total loss. She'd made new friends and enjoyed working with the people who had developed the project and brought it to life. Like most of the other bumps in the road of Erma's life, the demise of *Maggie* proved a sad but not personally devastating experience. When it was over, she turned in her rental car and headed happily back to the desert for good.

Critics may have had a hand in killing off *Maggie*, but they didn't hurt Erma then or ever. She respects critics and understands that they have a job to do. When her books are published, they are reviewed by publications ranging from *Publisher's Weekly* (the bible of the publishing industry) to *Library Journal* and dozens of local newspapers across the country. Erma reads her reviews, and she cares about what is said. She's interested in insightful views of her work but ignores flip remarks or superficial slaps that show how clever the writer thinks he is but reveal nothing useful. She understands that people will always take potshots at someone who is successful, especially someone who produces work perceived as "easy." Erma can spot critics who are thinking to themselves as they write, "I could do that a lot better than she does." She's learned to live with jealousy from those who believe her accomplishments are based on luck. Erma knows who she is and recognizes how hard she works. And she accepts the fact that not everyone loves her. She is convinced that if she criticized Adolph Hitler in a column, someone would accuse her of being insensitive.

It isn't critics, after all, who buy books. It's ordinary people who, by their requests, push nonfiction and novels alike to the top of the best-seller lists. These lists, compiled from bookstore sales, reflect the popularity of the authors whose works appear on them. The two lists considered the most authoritative in the United States are those appearing in *Publisher's Weekly* and *The New York Times*. The first best-seller lists included only fiction. Nonfiction was added in 1917. In 1976, paperback and hardcover sales were separated into two lists.

The New York Times listings are based on sales figures from over 3,000 bookstores and from wholesalers representing more than 28,000 other outlets.

In the mid-seventies, when the public first nibbled at Erma's offerings, a huge mega-hit book would sell 250,000 to 300,000 copies in hardcover. *The Grass Is Always Greener Over the Septic Tank* broke through with 500,000 copies. A year and a half later, *If Life Is a Bowl of Cherries, What Am I Doing in the Pits?* grabbed readers to the tune of 700,000 copies. Six hundred thousand copies of *Aunt Erma's Cope Book* sailed out of stores, and her biggest seller, 1983's *Motherhood: The Second Oldest Profession,* reached almost a million in hardcover sales.

Erma autographs books at a Chicago department store.

Today, the average hardcover book published in the United States sells 6,000 copies. A handful of authors like Stephen King and Danielle Steele might generate as many as 2 million hardcover sales, but they write fiction. Erma was ahead of the trend we're now experiencing where a small group of writers consistently sell extraordinary numbers. When she began, no nonfiction writer came close to matching her sales and, even now, few do.

8

The Writing Life

She reads every one of the 100 letters she receives each week. People write to Erma to share their own funny family stories or to explain to her how much her work means to them. They ask whether she'll speak to their local organization and when her next book is due to be published. Lots of letters are from people who want to become writers.

Generally, Erma explains how tough it is to break into humor writing but encourages them to pursue their dreams. Because Erma's writing sounds so natural, people assume it simply streams out of her mind onto paper. They imagine she writes as she's dusting or having lunch at the club with friends. They mention that they have "a few spare hours" and they think "writing your kind of stuff would be fun." Few people realize that Erma's work is more difficult than a full-time job. It requires total discipline and commitment.

That self-discipline, combined with a bad case of insecurity, has propelled Erma through more than twenty-five years of newspaper columns, over 3,000 of them. Amazingly, she's still stimulated and excited by the work. When a fresh idea strikes, she's like

Erma addressed the American Society of Newspaper Editors convention in 1989.

a little girl with a lacy new dress. She can hardly wait to "try it on," racing for the typewriter and tapping out the words at breakneck speed. Her friends claim Erma is "naturally funny." But she's not a stand-up comedian, eager for applause, who ladles out jokes like soup whenever she enters a room. Instead, she's a sponge, soaking up life's experiences, turning them upside down and making people laugh with recognition and even relief. Before Erma Bombeck, no one admitted that labor pain, potty training, and puppy love were funny. At least not in public.

Erma's humor stems from the absurdity she spies in everyday life. Over the years, she's relied on certain bread-and-butter ideas to generate columns and books—husbands, kids, housework, styles, and mothers. At first, words spilled from her head like rain. The writing was easy. But as Erma spurred a new awareness of household humor, other columnists entered the arena. She might still have taken the easy route, resting on her reputation as "the first" instead of struggling to remain the best. Instead, as Erma grew from isolated first-time mommy into world-famous author, her writing changed too. Increasingly, she began to write from the heart. Her words grew more personal, less brittle, more sensitive, and, she believes, better.

But as much as Erma may have changed and grown, her writing has always emphasized the human qualities we all share. People don't laugh at Erma Bombeck. They laugh with her. The root of her fans' unending support lies in shared experience.

When the name Erma Bombeck comes up, most people forget that her columns are often as poignant as they are funny. An editor once scolded her for injecting the heavier material. "You're not paid to be serious," he complained. But her fans disagreed. And as time went on and Erma gained more self-confidence, she realized that readers didn't come to her just for laughs. They craved her insights, her clear view of life's ups and downs. After all, life isn't 100 percent funny. Although Erma lays claim to the title of "world's greatest optimist," sometimes even she feels sad. She wants her readers to share that side too.

Her most popular columns are, in fact, the serious ones. The most requested one addresses three children and explains to each why "I've always loved you best." Another, titled "Time," reminds us to make every minute count by touching on those moments when the important things, like telling parents we love them, get buried in busy lives, often until it is too late. One of Erma's favorites, "Mother's Gift of Love," explains the logic that motivates mothers to act in ways children resent:

> I loved you enough to bug you about where you were going, with whom and what time you would get home.
>
> I loved you enough to be silent and let you discover that your friend was a creep.
>
> I loved you enough to make you return a Milky Way with a bite out of it to a drugstore and confess, 'I stole this.'

With all the popularity of these moving pieces, Erma claims the sentimental stories are easier to write. "Anybody," she contends, "can make you cry. But laughter, that's much more difficult."

Erma insists that most people—writers or not—have a few good columns inside, a few amusing incidents they could turn into stories, maybe even salable ones. But consistency without repeating, without boring the readers, involves strenuous mental work. The difficulty in achieving consistently interesting results has defeated most of Erma's competition, and there has been plenty. Some of the people who write to her eventually produce their own columns. Generally slanted to appeal to homegrown audiences, the columns run in local newspapers. A few have even gone on to syndication, but so far, none has matched Erma's popularity or her staying power.

When her children were small and they'd come home from school demanding attention, she'd tell them they'd have to wait. Writing came first. She felt guilty about it, but Erma always acted as though millions of people were depending on her, which, of course they were. She never let them down.

Some writers claim they suffer from writer's block— a kind of paralysis that overcomes them as they stare at a bare white sheet of paper. Erma doesn't believe in writer's block. She doesn't believe in missing deadlines. She doesn't believe in excuses.

She has turned out humor after a funeral and while hospitalized with kidney pain. In 1990, her stepfather died, and she spent four months flat on her back recovering from a herniated disc. She couldn't walk or sit at the typewriter. Her secretary brought a legal pad to her bedside so she could scratch out columns by hand. But, she says, no one cared. The syndicate didn't care and the readers didn't either. The space was reserved in hundreds of newspapers, and it had to be filled. "It doesn't matter how I feel," she says. "That's the worst part of this job. The constancy."

While Erma considers writer's block a luxury she can't afford, that doesn't mean she greets the blank pages enthusiastically every Monday morning. She lives for the days when an exciting idea hits. She'll dash into her office, crank paper into the IBM, and take off. But on bad days, she has no ideas. It seems as though there is nothing funny left in the world. As she mentioned in a *Good Housekeeping* magazine article in 1978, "I stare at that blank sheet of paper in the typewriter, and I think, 'Oh God, suppose I can't pull it off this time. Suppose I've lost the formula.' I die. I die a lot. And then I pull myself together and give it my best shot." On those days when fresh ideas are as scarce as diamonds, she delves into magazines and newspapers searching for stories that ignite her. She's not looking to copy anyone's ideas, just to get her thinking aimed in a direction from which she can take off on her own. And if worse comes to worst, she can always fall back on her old standbys, especially kids.

Some young people think Erma dislikes them because they are so often the target of her columns, but just the opposite is true. Humor requires a strong point of view. Erma writes as a parent. She loves kids and admires them. But she views their struggles from the perspective of an adult. And she thinks the ability to laugh at themselves can only help young people get through the tough times.

When she's struggling to nab an idea for a column, Erma might start by trying to recall if one of her own kids came by last week. If so, what did they do? If one wanted to borrow something, maybe there's an idea there—kids and borrowing. She'll jot down a couple of ideas, asking herself what kinds of things do they borrow? Money, cars, credit cards. And stretching things a bit—underwear, ice cream, the dog. Then she recalls her son asking constantly, "Do I have to pay for this with my own money?" Slowly the column takes shape.

Erma readily admits that not every column is prize-worthy, but vows that each is the best work she is capable of that day. And after filling space for so many years, she knows that no matter how bad the week, she'll come up with something.

It's impossible to write for twenty-five years and not repeat some relationships, themes, and topics. But she never takes the same tack or comes in the same door with them.

Erma can't sit around waiting for inspiration to strike. Stacks of clippings on topics that spark her imagination are piled on the shelves behind her desk, and she scribbles observations on a yellow legal pad or, if she's out of the house, on scraps of paper she jams in her purse. She catches ideas as easily as some people catch a cold. She's always on the lookout, alert to the amusing happening or the odd tidbit of information. Anyone but Erma Bombeck might read about the burglar who used a zucchini for a weapon to hold up a bank, chuckle, and forget it. To Erma, a story like that is gold just waiting to be mined. Erma clips the stories, and a few days, weeks, or months later, branded with her special comic touch, they may find their way into your newspaper. But her favorite columns are those that happen to her.

One day she joined her daughter at a Phoenix Suns basketball game. Betsy mentioned casually, "I just dropped my earring."

Erma said, "Fine, we'll look for it."

"You don't understand. I dropped it down the pants of the man in front of me."

That column practically wrote itself.

Ordinarily, columns require hours of thoughtful work and careful rewriting. Erma had joked that on her license, under "Occupation," she had listed, "Rewriter." Before those 450 words leave the house, they have been reread and polished and rewritten, "and then I want to run out to the mailbox and bring them back and do the whole thing again," Erma says. Even after two and a half decades of churning out columns, the majority don't come easily. First comes the lead, the opening that sets the tone for the column. The lead's snappy writing must lure readers in and let them know the column's subject. She writes this first, and if she can't get it right, she'll drop the idea and move on to something else. The entire column hinges on the first sentence or two. She doesn't outline a column and rarely knows where it will end. As the body of the piece begins to take shape, she notes ideas on a pad beside the typewriter for later insertion.

Once the column is born, she begins to shape it as a sculptor might, searching for the perfect words—dropping some, shuffling others. She plays with sentence length and reads the work out loud, seeking natural pauses that will make her unseen readers laugh. It's difficult to draw laughter from written words. When a comedian performs, "timing"—the delicate pauses between lines—initiates laughter. Comedians can take a story that wouldn't "read" funny and by manipulating facial expression, inflection, body language, and pauses, and injecting a healthy dose of "personality" have people rolling in the aisles. Readers must make do with an exclamation point in place of a raised eyebrow, a perfectly crafted sentence instead of a meaningful sigh.

Writers, though, do have some tricks that help. Adapting the basic methods of writing humorously creates the style for which each writer becomes known. Short sentences can be funny, and so can endless ones. Certain words make people laugh, especially when they are used in unexpected situations. When you are telling a joke, a few spare words here and there aren't too important. But in writing, an extra "and" can throw the reader off and kill the story.

Erma works to build each sentence to elicit the response she wants. She adds a pinch of exaggeration, a dab of surprise, a twist on the truth and glues them together with brisk, informal chatter that sustains reader interest to the end of the column.

But as hard as Erma works to make her writing crisp, clean, and funny, she admits to being mystified by what sometimes comes out unbidden. Occasionally, she'll be typing away and burst out laughing. Even as the words spring from under her fingers, she's not conscious of creating them. It's as if they are born in someone else's mind and she is the power line through which they flow. She has no control over them. Nor does she want any. Erma knows what's funny. She knows what works. Some days it's just easier than others to make it happen.

With her books, Erma depends on input from her longtime editor, Gladys Justin Carr, vice-president and associate publisher for HarperCollins trade book division. A lively chemistry unites two people who value each other as creators and critics. Gladys admits to laughing out loud at some of Erma's witty lines, rushing to share the bits of prose with whomever will listen. The two women share a collaborative relationship that many writers and editors would envy.

With their first project, *The Grass Is Always Greener Over the Septic Tank,* Gladys knew she was joining forces with a very special writer. Early on, when some critics dismissed Erma because her humor focused on home and family, Gladys sensed that there was a lot more to the writer than one-liners aimed at bratty kids and broken-down appliances. She encouraged Erma to explore the more sensitive side of humor, to examine both the laughter and the shadows that affect our lives. And while Erma might have one day done that on her own, having Gladys' support made the evolution easier. When she was doubtful, reassurance was only a phone call away. Gladys and Erma work together on almost every step of book production from the initial idea to marketing the finished product. They discuss the original concept, construction, voice, style, philosophy, and pacing. They negotiate through the creative stages, and sometimes, after all the work has paid off in a first draft, haggle over single words.

"Did you really mean that word?" Gladys will ask. Erma may pull out a dictionary in defense of her choice. They have engaged in four- or five-hour tugs-of-war over bits and pieces of Erma's prose. As the writer, Erma knows where she is coming from and where she wants to go. As the editor, Gladys can help her get there. But while Gladys may argue forcefully for her point of view, she knows that in the end, Erma's name will be on the book. Final decisions lie in the capable hands of the humorist.

Erma acknowledges run-ins with previous editors who misunderstood how written humor works—who wanted to make her sound like an English textbook. English textbooks aren't funny. As an English major, Erma knows the rules. She also chooses to break them. She uses contractions. She uses slang. She takes liberties with the language that make English teachers cringe. If she didn't, her writing wouldn't work.

Erma is a morning person, rising at 6:30 or 7:00 A.M. After trudging on a treadmill or dancing through an aerobics class, she gets to work. She's moved up from that plank balanced on cinder-blocks to an oak desk in a high-ceilinged room, a view of the desert valley spread below. A companionable green parrot sits quietly as Erma types, but squawks loudly at any interference. The room, with its multicolor rag rug, Mexican furnishings, shelves of books, papers, and photographs, seems to echo its owner's upbeat outlook on life.

Column writing consumes three weekdays. Her eleven-year *Good Morning America* stint required scripts sent two weeks before they were taped. She publishes a book every two years and devotes a year to writing each, squeezing time out of her work week or adhering to the workaholic lifestyle that she's followed her entire life. It takes enormous self-discipline to keep Erma out of her office on weekends.

Three days a week, a secretary helps with the mail and the numerous small but necessary tasks that have little to do with writing but a lot to do with being a writer. Erma does her own housework, shopping, and cooking. Her three children are grown now and on their own.

Although she has cut back in some areas, life can still grow hectic. Too many demands may crowd Erma's days, and she'll tell friends that she wants to quit. But even while the words are rolling off her tongue, she knows she won't do it. She has too much fun. She enjoys challenges and new ways to use her abilities, but she's also clear on what she wants and what she's best at. First and foremost, Erma sees herself as a writer, not a performer, and a long time ago she reached a point where she could reject projects even if they might mean enormous amounts of money.

Her agent, Aaron Priest, says that he's refused more money for her than most people will make in five lifetimes. She's been promised fortunes over the years to endorse products. In the early eighties, a television network executive offered Erma a one-hour daytime talk show. The package would have brought the writer hundreds of thousands of dollars. It would also have meant working under enormous pressure five days a week and inevitably would have allowed people to know her much more personally than this essentially private person was willing to accept. Priest turned it down. The gentlemen he was talking with were astounded.

"But you don't understand; we're offering eight figures," one started to say.

"No, you don't understand," replied Priest. "I understand numbers better than anyone you'll ever meet. . . . But what you have to understand is that if you took this desk and piled gold bars all the way up to the ceiling, if she didn't want to do it, it wouldn't make any difference."

Priest says, "Erma Bombeck is the one person I am absolutely positive you could not buy for any amount. If she didn't want to do it or didn't think it was right, you couldn't buy her." Through the years, Erma has been offered starring roles in everything from commercials to movies. She's never done any of them.

Aaron Priest respects Erma a great deal, and they agree, according to him, 99 percent of the time. They've argued long and hard over only one issue—Erma's refusal to produce a book of her best columns. Priest believes it would be a surefire success and that her fans would treasure a "Best of Bombeck" collection. Erma disagrees. She did it once (with *At Wit's End*), but now she's convinced that when people pay for a book, they deserve new material. Priest's opinion—they deserve something worthwhile, even if it's recycled. So far, Erma has won. Priest isn't betting that she'll change her mind.

9

Life Goes On

Erma had branched out from writing by producing a television series, stumping for the ERA, and even recording a comedy album (*The Family That Plays Together . . . Gets on Each Other's Nerves*). But never had she leaned further out on a limb than when she wrote *I Want to Grow Hair, I Want to Grow Up, I Want to Go to Boise.*

By 1986, Erma had sold several million books. Everyone thought they knew her. They knew what to expect from her writing. An Erma Bombeck book might contain some moving passages, but overall, she went for laughs. You could count on that.

I Want to Grow Hair, I Want to Grow Up, I Want to Go to Boise addressed a topic that was anything but funny—children with cancer. Erma seemed an unlikely candidate to write a book on such a serious topic. People wondered how she would handle the subject. Would her fans desert her when she deserted humor? Would the book sell? The doubters forgot that Erma hadn't stumbled into fame and fortune by accident. She had pursued her craft for a long time. She was a fine writer. And a good writer can tackle almost any subject, especially if she believes in it.

One day Erma received a letter from a woman she had never

met, Ann Wheat, assistant director of Arizona Childhood Cancer Services and director of Camp Sunrise (a camp for children with cancer) in northern Arizona. Ann invited Erma to lunch to discuss a project.

Wheat explained that a number of books had been published about children with cancer, but most ended when the child died. Yet, over the last two decades, the survival rate for childhood cancers had shot up. Twenty years ago, for instance, the number of children who lived through bouts with one form of cancer, acute lymphocytic leukemia, was zero. Now 60 percent of stricken children survive. Twelve years before, Camp Sunrise hadn't existed, neither had any of the seventy others that now provide fun and a stimulating camping environment for children with cancer. There weren't any camps twelve years before because there weren't any kids to go to them. But now that thousands of children every year were living with cancer, not dying from it, Ann Wheat thought they needed a booklet to make them laugh and give them hope.

At first, Erma couldn't imagine writing anything humorous about cancer. There had always been certain lines she had refused to cross as a humorist. She avoids hurtful or embarrassing jabs and scrupulously observes the limits of good taste. It wouldn't enter her mind to poke fun at war or child abuse. And she didn't think she could write humorously about cancer either. But Wheat refused to give up. She convinced Erma to visit Camp Sunrise, meet the children, and then decide.

Erma arrived at the camp weighed down with more than a suitcase. She carried a huge load of pity. That lasted about an hour. Some children looked quite healthy. Others were pale or limping or bald. But Erma heard laughter. She talked to some campers and discovered they were normal kids entirely free of self-pity. While battling the disease with fierce determination, they accepted the situation with a maturity that most adults found astonishing. They viewed cancer as an unwelcome visitor in their lives. It wasn't who they were. What cut deeper than the physical pain was the way healthy people treated them—as though, once touched by cancer, they were transformed, too fragile for fun. Some friends deserted them, others treated them as if they were somehow special. In either case, they hated it.

These kids knew the disease that attacked them. Some knew the odds against survival. They had faced pain, discouragement, and loss of dignity. They knew what they were missing, but they went on with their lives in the best way they could. At camp, that meant participating in all the traditional activities—with hair and limbs or without.

Erma knew then that these kids deserved more than a booklet. She had to write a book.

She set off on what was to be a monumental, emotionally exhausting journey. Things didn't start off well. When word got out that she was writing the book, she was deluged with thousands of letters from families that had been visited by cancer. People wanted to tell their stories from beginning to end. Their words were painful yet didn't touch on the small triumphs and the dark humor that was as much a part of the children's lives as chemotherapy and hair loss.

Despite feeling something was missing, Erma wrote three chapters and submitted them to a group of kids. She assumed they'd tell her what a wonderful job she'd done, how well she'd captured their experiences. Instead, they said, "Well, it's okay, but you've just got to make it funnier. This is not funny."

But unlike earlier books, Erma couldn't "make it funnier." The experiences had to come from the kids. And they were right. The surface stories, the ones they were often bursting to tell, weren't funny. It was only when Erma pushed past the recitation of shots and surgeries and painful treatments that children unearthed amusing incidents and helped Erma understand how humor made their lives bearable.

As she traveled the country meeting kids, families, and medical professionals, Erma's understanding and admiration grew.

For almost three years, she walked and talked and lived the life of families with cancer. She learned that with or without a serious illness, kids love to have fun. They want to be treated the same as everyone else, and they thrive on pranks, silliness, and practical jokes. A healthy child might thread rolls of toilet paper through the trees on her best friend's property. A child with cancer will twist the foot on his artificial leg so it faces the guy sitting behind him on the ski lift.

Time and again Erma saw that kids with cancer need to laugh. "If it hadn't been for my sense of humor," she heard over and over, "I wouldn't have survived this."

Erma says that before she wrote the book, she thought she knew everything there was to know about children, but meeting youngsters with cancer taught her new lessons about kids and about life. She thought a lot about what it meant to face a debilitating disease at such a young age. She discovered that children coping with cancer grew up quickly. They could spell "lymphoma" at an age when most youngsters still agonized over "house." They had lived with pain, fear, and disappointment, and it had made them appreciate everything life had to offer. Their attitude infected Erma. She tried to join them in finding joy in small things. She questioned the meaning of adulthood and wondered when she had allowed maturity to disguise the wonder she'd once felt at seeing sunsets and snowflakes.

From children with cancer, Erma, the humor writer, learned not to take life so seriously.

They also taught her that adults who stopped feeling superior, sat back, listened, and watched could benefit from the infinite wisdom of children who were battling every day of their lives. These children not only came through the darkest and most difficult times imaginable, but they also led their parents.

Her heart went out to these people. Childhood cancer victimizes the entire family. Guilt and blame tear parents apart. Erma saw, too, the price brothers and sisters paid. They got little attention and were sometimes sent to live with friends or relatives. Life in these families revolved around the sick child.

Everything about the book challenged Erma. Unlike her previous work, the words came hard. When she interviewed children, the braver they were, the more she cried. Although she understood that the book had to be funny, instead of calling on her emotions to lead the way, as she had in the past, she had to lay them aside. Yet she was forced to involve herself with the children and their families. She had to live their pain before she could understand their laughter.

Still, she was shocked by the humor the kids displayed and fearful of including it. If she joked about chemotherapy and missing limbs, wouldn't readers think her insensitive? But in the end she realized that the choice was not hers. She made no jokes about the kids. The kids joked about themselves. How could she fault them or refuse to include their material? Offending potential readers took a back seat to supporting the children's honest outlooks.

Eventually, after all the talking and visiting and crying and laughing and watching and listening, Erma found the book's voice. She didn't have to write a "funny" book. She didn't have to write a "serious" book. She had to write a book about life. And life isn't always happy and it isn't always sad, even for kids with cancer.

It turned out that *I Want to Grow Hair, I Want to Grow Up, I Want to Go to Boise* (the title was suggested by a boy's three wishes) was not so different from books Erma had written before. Parts of it tickled the funny bone and parts made readers cry.

Erma needn't have worried that readers would turn their backs when she tackled a more serious topic. While not a mega hit, the book made a great deal of money. She assigned all American profits

Erma accepts the American Cancer Society's Medal of Honor for her book, *I Want to Grow Hair, I Want to Grow Up, I Want to Go to Boise.*

from the book to the American Cancer Society. Profits from foreign editions go to Eleanor Roosevelt International Cancer Research Fellowships, which bring foreign cancer specialists to America to study cancer patients and treatments. Royalties on *I Want to Grow Hair, I Want to Grow Up, I Want to Go to Boise* have passed $1 million.

When the excitement surrounding the publication of the book subsided, Erma felt mentally, physically, and emotionally drained. Writing about children with cancer had changed her. She knew she would never be the same. But she was ready to return to writing the kind of books on which she had based her career. Her latest project, *When You Look Like Your Passport Photo, It's Time to Go Home*, is a throwback to her earlier exuberant, laughter-filled treats.

Erma's adventure travel vacations provided all the firsthand experience she needed for the book. She's crisscrossed the globe, visiting fifty-seven countries at last count, and will go almost anywhere to "get away from it all." Though the book might convince you that traveling is the last thing Erma Bombeck would enjoy, the truth is just the opposite. She likes nothing better than to round up a bunch of friends and family and set off for some exotic location.

When she's in Phoenix, she doesn't long for the whitewashed houses of Greece. She's a real homebody. Her house isn't so clean you could eat off the floor, but it's clean enough for her. She likes to putter around and work outside. The television gathers dust, but she loves to read, and needlework is a favorite hobby. A stack of books await at her bedside. She browses through the newspaper at night, finding the news too depressing to scan before morning writing sessions.

When she's away from home, Erma loves to shop. She claims she'll survey every floor of a big department store. "When I'm in New York, I have to keep myself from going in at sunrise and never coming out until it's dark," she once quipped in the *Ladies Home Journal* magazine.

While Erma has earned a black belt in shopping, she's also generous with family and friends and supports many worthy causes. She has steered fund raisers for her alma mater, the University of Dayton, as well as the Dayton YMCA. She helped launch an annual book fair, which has raised hundreds of thousands of dollars for kidney dialysis, transplants, and the cost of caring for people with kidney disease.

Over the years, Erma has become a public figure, yet she has always sheltered her personal life from public scrutiny.

No one watching a talk show featuring Erma learns much about the real Erma Bombeck. She'll joke and tease and exaggerate but rarely reveal important details. She zeroes in on her books or columns, or generalizes about women's lives, painting herself as "everywoman"—your average person living in a typical household. She plays the comedienne, the entertainer that she believes people want. "They really aren't all that interested in hearing about my real life," she says. "It's always been far too boring."

Erma's family remains at the center of her life. The stormy college years living at home gave way to a loving, supportive relationship between her and her mother who currently lives nearby. Erma claims that her mother charms or cajoles bookstore owners into moving her daughter's books to the front window. Her mother once said she was amazed by all Erma can do. Obviously she no longer regrets that her tap-dancing daughter never became another Shirley Temple.

The three Bombeck children are grown. They all managed to escape the ravages that often affect the kids of famous parents. Erma and Bill's bedrock values and determination to keep them out of the limelight, as well as retain their privacy, probably all contributed to their children's sense of self-worth.

Bill and Erma also took pains to help their children realize that they were important on their own, with or without a well-known mother. Living "in the sticks," where few reporters bothered to trek, helped the family avoid the public eye.

While her children were growing up, their perfectly normal behavior sparked Erma's mischievous slant on life. Other mothers cringed as their two-year-olds threw temper tantrums in the supermarket. Erma picked her toddler up, tucked him under her arm, dumped him in the car, and sped home to write about it. Through the years, the kids provided an unending stream of real-life adventures that left Erma's readers nodding their heads in sympathetic understanding.

Erma never singled out any of the three children in her columns.

Erma and her mother appear together with host Gary Collins on *Hour Magazine*.

She prefers to keep the kids in her columns and books faceless and general. She'll write, "my son" or "the four-year-old," leaving readers in doubt regarding the true identity of which Bombeck child actually threw up on his father as they toured the White House or which tearfully reported to the fourth grade class that his mother had eaten a pillowcase full of his Halloween candy.

If the humorous barbs at their lives upset the kids, Erma never knew about it. They didn't complain. She doubts they read many of the columns, and they understood that her stories were fictionalized. She never invaded their privacy or discussed their personal lives. Dating, finances, and problems were off limits. Not too long ago, though, she met a friend of Matt's who pointed out to Erma that a column she wrote about messy lockers ended up taped on her son's locker. She never knew. It bothers her that she may have caused him any pain.

When they were small, Erma feared the children might kill each other, but they have turned out to be best of friends. Not surprisingly, they all have a great sense of humor. As Erma says, "How could they live in this family for all those years and NOT have one?" Even now, when the Bombeck clan gathers, the house vibrates with laughter as the siblings poke fun at each other and their parents.

Betsy is currently a student at Arizona State University. Andy is a sixth grade teacher and Matt a TV writer. They agree that having Erma for a mother was terrific. She was a sensible and sensitive mother. Although she feels she neglected them sometimes when deadlines loomed or she had to fly off to publicize her latest creation, the children disagree. They insist she was there when they needed her.

By 1991, none of Erma's offspring had presented her with grandchildren. You can bet she is disappointed. It's not that she's anxious to hear a toddler shouting "Grandma!" No, she's anticipating the gold mine she'll uncover. Ten years' worth of columns at least, she figures.

Bill Bombeck has borne the weight of Erma's pointed jokes about "my husband" for forty-two years. Erma teases that she was married during a beer commercial to a man who never budges from the TV—even when she appeared once wearing a nightgown made of Astroturf. But Bill, who moved from teaching into school administration until he retired to manage the family's business affairs in 1978, has never been offended by his wife's frequent kidding in print.

Despite the barbs, the Bombeck marriage is solid and central to understanding who Erma Bombeck really is. Like any married couple, the two have their differences. An occasional shouting match echoes off the walls, but they have never faced a crisis that threatened to rip their marriage apart. They have never seriously considered separating. Bill was the only person Erma ever wanted to marry, and she's never for a moment doubted her choice. She understands that being the husband of a celebrity can be difficult. But Bill is a very secure man. Back in the days when men refused to "allow" their wives to work, he encouraged Erma to do whatever she needed to provide for her own happiness. It's obvious that Erma feels she owes Bill a debt for the enormous support he's given her dreams through the years. She can relax around Bill. They're not competitive. She doesn't have to be funny around him. Erma takes pains to surround herself with people who value Bill as much as they do her, who are interested in him as an individual, who laugh as much at his sense of humor as they do hers.

And if there is one thing Erma takes seriously, it's her marriage vows. "Marriage has no guarantees," she explains. "If that's what you're looking for, go live with a car battery."

Yes, Erma Bombeck takes marriage, motherhood, friendship, and writing seriously. It's life she finds so funny. And thank

Bill and Erma—still happy after forty-two years together.

goodness she does. For without her daffy glimpses of ourselves; without her irreverent pokes at the boring, the mundane, and the downright silly; without her hope, her joy, and her warmth, life would be a lot harder to take. She hasn't cured a dread disease or brought peace in our lifetime, but she's done something just as important. For most of her life, she's made the world laugh.

Chronology

1927—Erma Louise Fiste is born on February 21.

1936—Erma's father dies of a stroke.

1944—Erma graduates from high school.

1945—Erma goes to work full-time for the *Dayton Journal-Herald* newspaper as a copygirl, then leaves to attend Ohio University.

1949—Erma graduates from the University of Dayton with a B.A. in English. She returns to work at the *Dayton Journal-Herald* as a reporter.

Erma marries William Lawrence Bombeck.

1953—The Bombecks adopt Betsy, their first child. Erma leaves the *Dayton Journal-Herald*.

1955—Son Andrew is born.

1958—Son Matthew is born.

1964—Erma writes her first column for the *Kettering-Oakwood Times*.

1965—The *Dayton Journal-Herald* hires Erma to produce two columns a week.

Erma's column is syndicated by the Newsday syndicate.

1967—Erma's first book, *At Wit's End*, is published by Doubleday.

1971—*Just Wait Till You Have Children of Your Own*, co-authored with Bil Keane, is published by Doubleday.

1974—*I Lost Everything in the Post-Natal Depression* is published by Doubleday.

1976—*The Grass Is Always Greener Over the Septic Tank* is published by McGraw-Hill.

Erma begins twice a week segments on *Good Morning America*.

1978—Erma is appointed to the President's National Advisory Committee for Women.

She begins to campaign for the Equal Rights Amendment.

If Life Is a Bowl of Cherries, What Am I Doing in the Pits? is published by McGraw-Hill.

The Grass Is Always Greener Over the Septic Tank becomes a TV movie starring Carol Burnett.

1979—Erma's TV series, *Maggie*, is sold to ABC.

Aunt Erma's Cope Book is published by McGraw-Hill.

1983—*Motherhood: The Second Oldest Profession* is published by McGraw-Hill.

1986—Erma's columns are now syndicated in 900 newspapers and read by 30 million people.

Erma leaves *Good Morning America*.

1987—*Family: The Ties That Bind . . . and Gag!* is published by McGraw-Hill.

1989—*I Want to Grow Hair, I Want to Grow Up, I Want to Go to Boise* is published by Harper and Row.

1991—*When You Look Like Your Passport Photo, It's Time to Go Home* is published by HarperCollins.

Index

About the Author

Lynn Hutner Colwell is the author of over 100 articles for publications such as *Reader's Digest, Guideposts,* and *Family Circle.* Also a community relations specialist, Ms. Colwell lives with her family in Arizona. *Erma Bombeck: Writer and Humorist* is her first book for Enslow Publishers.